GETTING STARTED WITH LATIN

Beginning Latin for Homeschoolers and Self-Taught Students of Any Age

WILLIAM E. LINNEY

ARMFIELD ACADEMIC PRESS

IN MEMORIAM DR. CHARLOTTE HOGSETT

Gratias tibi ago

Armfield Academic Press
www.armfieldacademicpress.com

Editorial consultants: Ellen Boyer Correll, Sara Beatty
Editorial assistant: Geraldine Linney
Cover design: Janet Bergin

The image used to create the cover art for this book was provided
courtesy of Classical Numismatic Group, Inc. Specializing in ancient
Greek, Roman, Persian, Celtic, Byzantine, Jewish, Biblical, early Indian,
British, European medieval, and Renaissance coins and related
reference books.

www.cngcoins.com

ISBN-13: 978-0-9795051-0-2

ISBN-10: 0-9795051-0-0

Library of Congress Control Number: 2007903404

CONTENTS

PREFACE 4

HOW TO USE THIS BOOK 6

LESSONS 1–134 11

GENERAL ADVICE 165

ANSWER KEY 166

CLASSICAL PRONUNCIATION GUIDE 190

ECCLESIASTICAL PRONUNCIATION GUIDE 191

GLOSSARY 192

SUBJECT INDEX 193

PREFACE

Latin has fascinated and challenged me ever since my mother made me sign up for it in the tenth grade. From the first day of class I was intrigued by the way Latin words fit together like pieces of a puzzle. My interest was also stirred when I began to notice that a great number of English words come directly from Latin words. So even from the beginning, I had a strong appreciation for the Latin language—but at that young age I was unable to foresee the many ways in which Latin would enrich my life. Over the years my admiration of this language has continued to grow. And, with the added perspective that comes with getting older, I have a much deeper appreciation not only of the Latin language, but of education in general.

Consequently, when my sister asked me to teach beginning Latin to her two home-schooled children, I was delighted—until I remembered that my two prospective students would be on their own most of the time because of the great distance separating us. After giving it some thought, I realized that having the right textbook would be crucial for making long-distance teaching a success. With this in mind, I began to search for the perfect beginning Latin method. As I searched, I pictured in my mind a book that would...

- Be self-explanatory, self-paced, self-contained, and inexpensive
- Allow the student to make progress with or without a Latin teacher
- Provide plenty of practice exercises after each new concept so the student can master each idea before moving on to the next one
- Avoid making beginning Latin any more difficult than it actually is

However, after examining many books, I reluctantly admitted to myself that the book I had pictured in my mind did not exist. Therefore, because I was completely ignorant of how difficult it is to write a book, I set out to write my own beginning Latin method.

Getting Started with Latin was created to meet the unique needs of homeschooled and self-taught students. I designed this book to meet not only my criteria, but the recommendations of several experienced homeschool mothers. They urged me to make my beginning Latin method completely self-contained, with no extra materials to purchase (such as pronunciation recordings, answer keys, or teachers' editions). They even asked that the book be in a large format to make it easier to use, as well as non-consumable so they could use it with multiple children. I have tried to accommodate these and other requests by putting the answer key in the back of the book and by providing free pronunciation recordings, available for download at www.gettingstartedwithlatin.com.

In this method, new words and concepts are introduced in a gradual yet systematic fashion. Each lesson provides many exercises for practicing the new material while reviewing material from previous lessons. And, just to make things interesting, every once in a while you will run into a page entitled Latin Expressions. These brief and often humorous commentaries will explain the meanings of the Latin sayings you have seen for years but never had a clue as to their meaning.

Getting Started with Latin makes beginning Latin accessible by gently lifting the student over some of the obstacles that can make Latin seem out of reach. Because this book moves so gradually, students probably will not say, "This is too hard for me. I quit!" Instead, these bite-size lessons should leave the student encouraged and ready to move forward all the way to the end of the book. But when you do finish this book, don't let your Latin studies end there. This book only covers the beginning stages of Latin grammar. I am confident that if this book causes you to grasp the beauty and power of Latin, even in some small way, you will have no trouble finding the motivation to continue your studies at the next level.

William E. Linney

HOW TO USE THIS BOOK

This book is structured around one main teaching method: Teach one concept at a time and let the student master that concept before introducing the next one. With that in mind, read the tips listed below to help you use this book to the greatest advantage.

THE NEW WORD

Start each lesson by observing the new word for that particular lesson. All Latin words in this book are in **bold print** so they will be easy to recognize. The meaning of the new word is in *italics*. In some lessons you will learn a new concept and in others you will simply review material from previous lessons.

PRONUNCIATION

The best way to learn correct pronunciation is by listening and copying what you hear. Visit www.gettingstartedwithlatin.com to download the free pronunciation recordings in MP3 format. In these recordings, each new word and exercise is read aloud by the author. You may listen to them on your computer, tablet, smart phone, or other device. Choose from either classical or ecclesiastical (church) pronunciation recordings. Either way, these free audio recordings will help you to achieve proper Latin pronunciation. And, as you improve, you will be able to translate the exercises as you hear them read aloud by the author.

Occasionally, there will be a written pronunciation tip at the beginning of a particular lesson. These tips are included in the book to prevent some of the most common pronunciation errors. These written pronunciation tips explain how a word will be pronounced in both classical and ecclesiastical style. To further assist you in achieving proper pronunciation, there are two pronunciation charts at the end of the book.

Many of the homeschool mothers I have met and worked with seem to be very concerned about Latin pronunciation. They are worried that they will somehow cause permanent damage to their child's intellect if they mispronounce Latin vowels or if they choose to emulate the wrong style of pronunciation. Please allow me to address this issue: Classical pronunciation is the style of pronunciation used in the Latin departments of most colleges and universities. Latin scholars use this type of pronunciation because it is supposed to reflect accurately the way Latin was pronounced by the ancient Romans. Ecclesiastical (church) pronunciation, on the other hand, is the style of pronunciation used by the Roman Catholic Church. Roman Catholic students may want to employ this type of pronunciation because they may have the opportunity to use it in the recitation of prayers or in other religious activities.

Regardless of which pronunciation style you choose, please don't lose any sleep over it. Of course you should do your best to pronounce the words correctly. But please remember that if you do mispronounce a word, you will not ruin your child's education. And, the Latin Police will not come to your home and arrest you.

GRAMMATICAL INFORMATION

If needed, a lesson may contain an explanation of how to use the new word introduced in that lesson. Charts and examples will be used to give the reader a clear presentation of the Latin grammar knowledge needed for that particular lesson.

THE EXERCISES

Armed with the knowledge of the new word and how to use it, the student should then begin to translate the exercises. In a homeschool environment, it is probably best to have students write their answers in a notebook. Older students and adults may prefer to do the exercises mentally. Next, turn to the answer key in the back of the book to see if your translations are correct. By comparing the Latin and the English, you will be able to learn from your mistakes. Translating the exercises over and over (even memorizing them) will enhance learning and speed progress.

SPEAKING LATIN

If I could recommend any one particular thing that could help you learn Latin faster and more easily, it would be to speak the Latin language every day. Yes, you read that correctly—I said to speak Latin. This advice might sound unusual to you because unlike modern languages such as French, German, or Chinese, Latin is no longer spoken as a national language. And we can't travel back in time to talk to the ancient Romans, either. However, from an educational perspective, there are many benefits to speaking Latin.

If you only read Latin and translate it into English, your experience with Latin will be limited. When you translate Latin, here is the sequence of events: 1) You see a Latin word. 2) You try to think of the English equivalent of that word. 3) When the English equivalent pops into your head, it brings with it the meanings, thoughts, and feelings associated with it. This kind of exercise really is focused on English, not Latin, because the goal becomes to get the English words right. Sure, you start out with Latin, but everything ends up as English.

But when you speak Latin, your mind remains focused on Latin. Since you can't depend on English to express yourself verbally, you must keep the Latin words you know in the forefront of your mind, using them to formulate thoughts and create meaningful sentences. And as you speak Latin more and more, you will begin to associate images, thoughts, and feelings with the Latin words themselves, not just with their English equivalents. This will help you to form a more direct, intimate connection with the Latin language.

So as you go through this book, don't just read and translate the exercises—also incorporate speaking and listening into your daily study habits. There are several ways to do this. One way is to have conversations in Latin with another person such as a teacher, parent, family member, or fellow student. You can talk about the things that happen in the exercises in the book, or you can do role-playing exercises in which you pretend to be one of the people in the exercises. If you have no one to talk to, don't worry—you can still do something called *narration*. Narration is, more or less, talking to yourself. You can read some exercises in Latin and then begin to talk about them out loud, retelling or restating what happened. You can pretend to be one of the characters in the exercises and speak in the first person. Another useful technique is to close your eyes and see the story in your mind's eye while you narrate what is happening in Latin.

Above all, don't think of Latin as a museum exhibit that sits inside a glass display case—something that can only be looked at but never touched or handled. Instead, try to view Latin as something that you can pick up, touch, examine—even play with. Don't be afraid to make mistakes! Mistakes are an important part of the learning process. Roll up your sleeves and jump fully into the Latin language, and you will experience the language in a more fulfilling and satisfying way.

LATIN COMPOSITION

In addition to speaking Latin, you can also do what is called *Latin composition*. That's when you take some idea and try to write it out in correct Latin. Figuring out how to write something in Latin can be a great learning tool because, like speaking Latin, it requires you to focus on Latin, not English. Try it and see! Again, it is probably best to write these Latin composition exercises in a notebook.

DON'T PUT THE CART BEFORE THE HORSE

Do not skip ahead to a future lesson. Because each lesson builds directly on the preceding lessons, the student should do the lessons in the order given. If you start to feel lost or confused, back up a few lessons and review. Or, take a break and come back to the material at a later time. Remember that review and repetition are essential when learning any language. One of the best things you can do to improve your understanding of Latin is to review the lessons repeatedly.

LATIN EXPRESSIONS

Latin sayings and expressions are everywhere! Where did all these expressions come from? What do they mean? In this book, every few lessons you will find a page entitled Latin Expressions. These short explanations of some of the most common Latin expressions are meant to inform the student while stimulating further interest in Latin.

STAY FLEXIBLE

Everyone has a different learning style, so use this book in ways that fit your needs or the needs of your students. You can learn Latin as a family, on your own, or in a homeschool environment. Be creative! You could even have one night of the week where the entire family is only allowed to speak Latin. You may even think of a way to use this book that no one else has thought of (putting it under the short leg of the kitchen table does not count).

TESTS AND QUIZZES

To give a student a test or quiz, simply back up to a previous lesson. Have the student translate those exercises without looking at the answers. Then, the teacher or parent can grade the exercises using the answers in the back of the book. Another possibility would be to test the student's listening skills by having him or her translate the exercises directly from the audio recording for that lesson.

SCHEDULING

Some homeschool parents like a lot of structure in their teaching schedules, while others prefer a less structured learning environment. Depending on your personal preferences, you may either plan to cover a certain number of lessons in a certain period of time, or allow your students to determine their own pace. It's up to you.

HOW MUCH TIME PER DAY?

A few minutes a day with this book is better than longer, less frequent sessions. Thirty minutes a day is ideal for language study. Of course, this may vary with each student's age, ability, and needs.

SELF-TAUGHT ADULTS

Adults who use this book will enjoy the freedom of learning Latin whenever and wherever they please. High school and college students can use it to get a head start before taking a Latin class, to satisfy curiosity, or to try something new. Busy adults can use it to study at lunchtime, break time, or while commuting to work (as long as someone else is driving the vehicle). The short lessons in this book will fit any schedule.

SURF THE NET

The website that accompanies this book (www.gettingstartedwithlatin.com) has free resources to aid you in your study of Latin. Be sure to check it out!

LESSON ONE

NEW WORD   **nauta**

MEANING   *sailor*

PRONUNCIATION TIP: In both classical and ecclesiastical pronunciation, **nauta** has two syllables. The first syllable sounds like the English word *now*. In a two-syllable word, the accent always goes on the first syllable.

Latin pronunciation is not the same as English pronunciation. The best way to learn correct pronunciation is by listening. Be sure to visit www.gettingstartedwithlatin.com to download the free pronunciation recordings in MP3 format. Choose either classical or ecclesiastical (church) pronunciation recordings. In these free audio recordings, each word and exercise is read aloud by the author. You may listen to these recordings on your computer, tablet, smart phone, or MP3 player. You can even burn them to a CD and listen to them on any CD player.

To further assist you in achieving proper pronunciation, there are pronunciation charts at the end of the book for reference.

LESSON TWO

NO "THE" IN LATIN

In Latin, there are no words for *the*, *a*, or *an*. Depending on the way it is used in a sentence, the word **nauta** could mean *sailor*, *a sailor*, or *the sailor*. When you translate Latin into English, you must decide on your own where to put in words like *the*, *a*, and *an*.

LESSON THREE

NEW WORD   **sum**

MEANING   *I am*

In English, it takes two words to say *I am*. In Latin, it takes only one: **sum**.

EXERCISES:

1. **Sum.**
2. **Sum nauta.**

When you see the exercises in each lesson, try to translate them on your own. The answers are in the back of the book to keep you from peeking.

The answers to this lesson are on page 166.

LESSON FOUR

WORD ORDER

The words in a Latin sentence are not usually in the same order as they would be in an English sentence. For example, **sum nauta** and **nauta sum** mean the same thing. This may seem strange to you at first, but it will become easier with practice.

EXERCISES:

1. **Sum nauta.**
2. **Nauta sum.**

Answers on page 166.

LATIN EXPRESSIONS

Have you ever wondered what **cogito ergo sum** means?

Cogito means *I think*. **Ergo** means *therefore* (don't confuse **ergo** with **ego**). **Sum**, as you already know, means *I am*. So, **cogito ergo sum** literally means *I think, therefore I am*.

This expression comes from the great French philosopher, scientist, and mathematician René Descartes (pronounced *day-KART*). Descartes reasoned that by his own act of doubting he could be sure of his own existence. This idea is captured by the Latin expression **cogito ergo sum**.

Speaking of Latin, the Latin version of Descartes' name is **Cartesius**. So anything pertaining to Descartes is referred to as *Cartesian*.

13

LESSON FIVE

NEW WORD   **ego**

MEANING   *I*

PRONUNCIATION TIP: In both classical and ecclesiastical pronunciation, **ego** is pronounced like the English word *egg* but with an *o* sound added to the end.

Sum means *I am* by itself. However, **ego** may also be used with **sum**. Whether you say **sum** or **ego sum**, it still just means *I am*. **Ego** is often used for emphasis.

Remember: The words in a Latin sentence may be in an unusual order.

EXERCISES:

1. **Sum.**
2. **Ego sum.**
3. **Sum nauta.**
4. **Nauta sum.**
5. **Ego sum nauta.**
6. **Ego nauta sum.**
7. **Nauta ego sum.**

Answers on page 166.

14

LESSON SIX

NEW WORD   **agricola**

MEANING   *farmer*

PRONUNCIATION TIP: If you are using the ecclesiastical style of pronunciation, remember to roll the *r* in **agricola** lightly.

EXERCISES:

1. **Sum agricola.**
2. **Agricola sum.**
3. **Ego sum agricola.**
4. **Ego agricola sum.**
5. **Sum nauta.**
6. **Nauta sum.**
7. **Ego nauta sum.**
8. **Nauta ego sum.**

Answers on page 166.

LESSON SEVEN

SUBJECTS

A noun is a person, place, or thing. The subject of a sentence is the noun that is doing the action in the sentence. In the Latin exercises you have seen so far, the subject of the sentence has always been *I*. Soon you will learn to read more complex Latin sentences.

For practice, see if you can identify the subject of each of the following sentences.

EXERCISES:

1. I am.
2. You are.
3. She is tall.
4. On Tuesdays and Thursdays, Fred likes to go jogging.
5. Chicago is a big city.
6. The children have ice cream cones.
7. The car has a flat tire.
8. My oatmeal is too hot.
9. Switzerland is a beautiful country.
10. In the winter, Grandfather always wears his old brown coat.

Answers on page 166.

LESSON EIGHT

NEW WORD   **et**

MEANING   *and*

Most of the time, **et** simply means *and*. But if you use it twice, it can mean *both...and*. Here is an example:

> **Sum et nauta et agricola** *(I am both a sailor and a farmer).*

EXERCISES:

1. **Nauta et agricola**
2. **Agricola et nauta**
3. **Ego sum nauta.**
4. **Nauta sum.**
5. **Et agricola et nauta sum.**
6. **Ego sum et nauta et agricola.**

Answers on page 166.

LESSON NINE

VERBS

In lesson 7 you learned to recognize the subject of a sentence. Now let's move on to verbs. Verbs are words that tell us what the subject of a sentence is doing. Verbs can be action words such as *dance, shout, walk, talk,* or *write.* Or, they can be verbs of being or existing such as *is, are, was, were,* and *will be.* Verbs of being are also called *linking verbs.*

See if you can identify the subject and verb of each of the following sentences.

EXERCISES:

1. She walks to school every day.
2. My car is dirty.
3. I see a quarter on the ground.
4. Yesterday he bought a trumpet.
5. Sam loves chocolate milk.
6. They swim in the pool every day.
7. The books are heavy.
8. I called Aunt Martha last week.
9. China produces a lot of green tea.
10. Mr. Smith's dog barks at night.

Answers on page 166.

LESSON TEN

NEW WORD **nōn**

MEANING *not*

PRONUNCIATION TIP: In both classical and ecclesiastical pronunciations, **nōn** rhymes with *bone, loan,* and *tone.*

In a sentence, **nōn** usually comes immediately before the verb. For example, **nōn sum** means *I am not.*

EXERCISES:

1. **Nōn sum.**
2. **Ego nōn sum.**
3. **Nōn sum nauta.**
4. **Nauta nōn sum.**
5. **Ego agricola nōn sum.**
6. **Agricola ego nōn sum.**
7. **Sum et nauta et agricola.**
8. **Et agricola et nauta ego sum.**

Answers on page 167.

LESSON ELEVEN

NEW WORD   **es**

MEANING   *you are*

In English, it takes two words to say *you are*. In Latin, it takes only one: **es**. **Es** is used only when speaking to one person.

EXERCISES:

1. **Es.**
2. **Nōn es.**
3. **Es agricola.**
4. **Agricola es.**
5. **Nōn es agricola.**
6. **Agricola nōn es.**
7. **Sum agricola.**
8. **Ego nōn sum nauta.**
9. **Es et nauta et agricola.**
10. **Nauta sum et agricola es.**

Answers on page 167.

LESSON TWELVE

NEW WORD   **poēta**

MEANING   *poet*

EXERCISES:

1. **Es poēta.**
2. **Poēta es.**
3. **Nōn es poēta.**
4. **Poēta nōn es.**
5. **Sum et agricola et poēta.**
6. **Et nauta et agricola sum.**
7. **Ego sum nauta.**
8. **Nōn es nauta.**
9. **Poēta ego nōn sum.**
10. **Agricola sum et poēta es.**

Answers on page 167.

LATIN EXPRESSIONS

The abbreviation **etc.** seems to be everywhere. What does it mean?

This common abbreviation is short for the Latin words **et cetera. Et,** as you already know, means *and.* **Cetera** is an adjective (in plural form) that means *the remaining things.* So when you say **et cetera,** you are saying *and the rest* or *and the others.* Sometimes **et cetera** is mispronounced **ec cetera.** But as a student of Latin, you know better!

LESSON 13

NEW WORD   **est**

MEANING   *he is*

In English, it takes two words to say *he is*. In Latin, it takes only one: **est**. **Est** can also mean *she is* and *it is*, but for now just translate **est** as *he is*.

EXERCISES:

1. **Est poēta.**
2. **Poēta est.**
3. **Est nauta.**
4. **Nauta est.**
5. **Nōn est agricola.**
6. **Nōn es nauta.**
7. **Agricola nōn es.**
8. **Ego nōn sum.**
9. **Et agricola et poēta sum.**
10. **Ego nauta nōn sum.**

Answers on page 167.

LESSON 14

MORE ABOUT EST

Let's learn another way to use **est**. Sometimes **est** simply means *is*. Consider the following example:

Poēta est agricola.

This sentence means *the poet is a farmer*. Here, it is clear that **poēta** is the subject of the sentence. Therefore, we leave out *he* and **est** simply means *is*.

In other cases, there is no other word to be the subject of the sentence, as in the following example:

Poēta est.

This sentence means *he is a poet*. Here it is clear that there is no other word available to be the subject of the sentence. So, we translate **est** as *he is*.

If you cannot figure out whether **est** means *is* or *he is*, try them both. The correct meaning of **est** should become clear.

EXERCISES:
1. **Agricola est poēta.**
2. **Nauta est poēta.**
3. **Est nauta.**
4. **Poēta nōn est nauta.**
5. **Nauta nōn est.**
6. **Poēta est agricola.**
7. **Nauta nōn est agricola.**
8. **Nōn es poēta.**
9. **Ego agricola nōn sum.**
10. **Es et agricola et poēta.**

Answers on page 167.

23

LESSON 15

SINGULAR AND PLURAL

Singular means one of something.

Plural means more than one of something.

In the exercises below, try to figure out what the subject of the sentence is. Then, decide if the subject is singular or plural.

EXERCISES:

1. The car is red.
2. We have ice cream cones.
3. Flowers are pretty.
4. I like blueberry pie.
5. They like hamburgers.
6. Jimmy will go to school tomorrow.
7. The team has five players.
8. Mary is a good clarinet player.
9. In France, they speak French.
10. Many houses are on our street.

Answers on page 167.

LESSON 16

NEW WORD   **nautae**

MEANING   *sailors*

PRONUNCIATION TIP: In classical pronunciation, the *ae* at the end of **nau-tae** sounds like the English word *eye*. In ecclesiastical pronunciation, the *ae* at the end of **nautae** sounds like the *e* in *bet*.

Nautae is your first plural word in Latin. **Nauta** becomes plural when we change the ending from **-a** to **-ae**. The same rule applies to **agricola** and **poēta**.

EXERCISES:

1. What is the plural form of **agricola** ?
2. What is the plural form of **poēta** ?

Answers on page 167.

LESSON 17

NEW WORD   **sumus**

MEANING   *we are*

When studying any language it is important to notice whether each individual word is singular or plural. Why? Because each word in a sentence must interact correctly with the words around it. In grammatical terms, this is called *agreement*. See if you can figure out what is wrong with the following example:

> **Sum agricolae.**

Did you notice something strange about that sentence? This sentence does not make any sense because it means *I am farmers*. In other words, **sum** and **agricolae** do not agree because **sum** is singular and **agricolae** is plural. A correct sentence would be **sum agricola** because **sum** and **agricola** agree. Again, see if you can figure out what is wrong with the following example:

> **Sumus agricola.**

This sentence does not make any sense either because it means *we are a farmer*. **Sumus** and **agricola** do not agree because **sumus** is plural and **agricola** is singular. A correct sentence would be **sumus agricolae** because **sumus** and **agricolae** agree.

EXERCISES:

1. **Sumus.**
2. **Sumus nautae.**
3. **Nautae sumus.**
4. **Agricolae nōn sumus.**
5. **Nōn sumus agricolae.**
6. **Sumus agricolae et poētae.**
7. **Poēta nōn es.**
8. **Ego sum poēta.**
9. **Poēta est nauta.**
10. **Nauta est.**

Answers on page 168.

LESSON 18

NEW WORD   **estis**

MEANING   *you are* (plural)

You already know that the word **es** means *you are*. We use **es** when speaking to one person. **Estis** also means *you are*, but with one important difference: **estis** is plural. The English word *you* can refer to one person or more than one person. Other languages (such as Latin) have different words for singular *you* and plural *you*.

Sometimes we use such as *you guys* or *you people* to try to make it clear that we are talking to more than one person. In the southeastern United States, where this author is from, we often use the contraction *y'all* to address more than one person (never just one). *Y'all* is simply a contraction of the words *you* and *all*. *Y'all* rhymes with *hall*, *ball* and *fall*.

Some teachers use the word *y'all* to help students understand the difference between **es** and **estis**. So, in the answer key, **estis** will be translated as *y'all are*. If you are from the southeastern United States, using this word will be easy for you. If not, y'all will get used to it after using it a few times. Either way, try to have fun with it and don't take it too seriously.

EXERCISES:
1. **Estis.**
2. **Estis agricolae.**
3. **Agricolae estis.**
4. **Poētae nōn estis.**
5. **Sumus poētae et estis nautae.**
6. **Et nautae et poētae estis.**
7. **Poēta nōn es.**
8. **Agricola est poēta.**
9. **Poēta ego sum.**
10. **Est nauta.**

Answers on page 168.

LESSON 19

NEW WORD   **sunt**

MEANING   *they are*

Sunt is very similar to **est**. **Sunt** can mean *they are* or just *are*. Consider the following example:

> **Agricolae sunt poētae.**

This sentence means *the farmers are poets*. Here it is clear that **agricolae** is the subject of the sentence. Therefore, we leave out *they* and **sunt** simply means *are*.

In other cases, there is no other word to be the subject of the sentence, as in the following example:

> **Poētae sunt.**

This sentence means *they are poets*. Here there is no other word available to be the subject of the sentence. So, we translate **sunt** as *they are*.

Again (just as with **est**), if you cannot figure out whether **sunt** means *are* or *they are*, try them both. The correct meaning of **sunt** should become clear.

EXERCISES:
1. **Poētae sunt.**
2. **Poētae sunt agricolae.**
3. **Agricolae nōn sunt.**
4. **Poētae sunt nautae.**
5. **Poēta est.**
6. **Estis poētae.**
7. **Nautae nōn sunt agricolae.**
8. **Agricola est poēta.**
9. **Nautae sumus.**
10. **Nōn es poēta.**

Answers on page 168.

LESSON 20

MEMORIZATION

Let's put all the verbs you know into a chart to help you remember them.

sum	sumus
es	estis
est	sunt

When studying any language, it is very beneficial to memorize groups of verbs such as this one. To help you remember these verbs, say them over and over in this sequence: **sum**, **es**, **est**, **sumus**, **estis**, **sunt**. Students of Latin often chant or sing groups of verbs like this. You or your students may enjoy making up your own games, songs, or chants to help you memorize things more easily.

LATIN EXPRESSIONS

Have you ever seen the abbreviations **i.e.** and **e.g.**?

The abbreviation **i.e.** is short for **id est**. **Id**, in this case, means *that*. You already know that **est** means *is*. Literally, **id est** means *that is*. Writers use this expression to further clarify a general statement. When you see this term you can take it to mean *that is to say* or *in other words*. Here is an example of how **i.e.** is used in a sentence:

> The church needed someone who knew how to repair things (**i.e.**, a handyman).

The abbreviation **e.g.** is short for **exempli gratia**. **Gratia** means *for the sake*. **Exempli** means *of an example*. So literally, **exempli gratia** means *for the sake of an example*. Writers use this term to give specific examples of a more general thing they have already mentioned. Here is how **e.g.** is used in a sentence:

> Some of the most nutritious foods a person can eat are green, leafy vegetables (**e.g.**, spinach).

LESSON 21

PERSON

We have already covered singular and plural. Now let's talk about another quality that verbs have. In Latin, verbs tell not only what action is taking place, but also who is performing the action. Verbs can be in the first person, second person, or third person.

❑ Verbs that refer to *I* or *we* are first person (the person who is speaking).

❑ Verbs that refer to *you*, either singular or plural, are second person (the person or people to whom the speaker is speaking). In this book we will use *y'all* for the second person plural to help distinguish it from the second person singular.

❑ Verbs that refer to *he, she, it,* or *they* are third person (the person, thing, people, or things being spoken about).

The following chart should help illustrate this concept:

	SINGULAR	PLURAL
FIRST PERSON	I	we
SECOND PERSON	you	you *y'all*
THIRD PERSON	he, she, it	they are

31

If we put all the Latin verbs you know in a chart like the one above, it would look like this:

	SINGULAR	PLURAL
FIRST PERSON	**sum**	**sumus**
SECOND PERSON	**es**	**estis**
THIRD PERSON	**est**	**sunt**

Remember to chant or sing these verbs over and over in order to memorize them.

In the exercises below, determine what the subject of each sentence is. Then, determine if it is first person, second person, or third person. Finally, determine whether it is singular or plural.

EXERCISES:

1. I am hungry.
2. You are a nice person.
3. She is very smart.
4. We are going to the park.
5. Y'all have a beautiful home.
6. They eat lunch at Aunt Martha's house every Sunday.
7. He is a tennis player.
8. It is a history book.
9. Y'all really know how to throw a party.
10. The flowers in your garden are pretty.

Answers on page 168.

L E S S O N 2 2

DIRECT OBJECTS

A direct object is a noun that is the target of the action being performed by the subject of the sentence. Here is an example:

Harold plays the drums.

In this sentence, the word *drums* is the direct object. Here is another example:

Helen ate the orange.

In this sentence, the word *orange* is the direct object. See if you can find the direct object in each of the exercises below:

EXERCISES:

1. Mr. Jones bought a newspaper.
2. I will see a movie tomorrow.
3. Harry is playing the trombone.
4. On Saturday, we will play baseball.
5. James caught a fish.
6. They accidentally broke the radio.
7. Y'all painted the wrong building.
8. Yesterday we listened to a long speech.
9. Mr. Underwood lost his wallet.
10. Geraldine saw a deer in the woods.

Answers on page 168.

LESSON 23

DIRECT OBJECTS (THIS TIME IN LATIN)

When **nauta** is the subject of a sentence it appears in its normal form which is **nauta**. When **nauta** is the direct object in a sentence, we change the ending to -**am**. That makes it **nautam** instead of **nauta**. Use **nautam** only with action verbs, not verbs of being or existing like *am, are,* or *is* (also called *linking verbs).* A word that renames the subject of the sentence after a verb of being is called a *predicate nominative.* Predicate nominatives take the normal form of the word, not the direct object form. Here are some examples to help illustrate these concepts:

> The **nauta** saw an island.

In this sentence, *sailor* is the subject of the sentence, so it retains its normal form which is **nauta**. Here is another example:

> I saw a **nautam**.

In this sentence, *sailor* is the direct object, so the ending changes to -**am** to make **nautam**. Here is a third example:

> The man is a **nauta**.

In this sentence, *sailor* is a predicate nominative. The verb here is a verb of being, not an action verb. A verb of being cannot produce a direct object—only an action verb can do that. Therefore **nauta** retains its normal form which is **nauta**.

In the exercises below, fill in the blank with either **nauta** or **nautam**. Then, give the reason for your choice. Choose from among the following three reasons:

- Because it is the subject of the sentence
- Because it is the direct object of the sentence
- Because it is a predicate nominative

Write your answers in your notebook or on a separate sheet of paper.

EXERCISES:

1. Yesterday, I saw a _____ down at the dock.
2. I am a _____ .
3. A _____ steered the ship into the harbor.
4. I hired a _____ to help us steer the boat.
5. A _____ walked toward the ship.
6. The _____ is very strong.
7. I watched the _____ as he lowered the anchor.
8. He is a _____ .
9. You helped the _____ with the rope.
10. I will be a _____ someday.

Answers on page 168.

LATIN EXPRESSIONS

Knowing the difference between A.M. and P.M. is very important. If you get them mixed up, you could be twelve hours late (or early)!

A.M. and P.M. are abbreviations for two meaningful Latin expressions. A.M. stands for **ante meridiem** and P.M. stands for **post meridiem**. **Meridiem** is a form of the word **meridies** which means *noon* or *midday*. **Ante** means *before*. **Post** means *after*. So, **ante meridiem** literally means *before noon* and **post meridiem** means *after noon*.

According to the Roman author Varro, the word **meridies** used to be spelled **medidies**. **Medidies** is a compound word made up of the words **dies** and **medius**. **Dies** (pronounced *DEE-ace*) means *day*. The prefix **medi-** is short for **medius** which means *middle*. So **medidies**, the older form of the word, means the *middle of the day*. So when you say A.M. you are really saying *before the middle of the day*, and when you say P.M. you are really saying *after the middle of the day*. But it's a lot easier just to say A.M. and P.M.

LESSON 24

NEW WORD   spectō

MEANING   *I watch, I do watch, I am watching*

Spectō is our first action verb in Latin. It means *I watch, I do watch,* or *I am watching*. You can use words such as **ego** and **nōn** along with **spectō**, just as you would with **sum**.

In the last lesson, we learned that if **nauta** is a direct object, the ending changes to **-am**. This rule is also true for **agricola** and **poēta**. **Agricola** becomes **agricolam** and **poēta** becomes **poētam**. Keep this in mind as you translate the exercises into English. Don't let the order of the words confuse you. Instead, just focus on the function of each individual word.

Since **spectō** can mean *I watch, I do watch,* or *I am watching*, you must decide on your own which one sounds best when you translate the exercises into English.

EXERCISES:

1. **Spectō nautam.**
2. **Nautam spectō.**
3. **Nōn spectō agricolam.**
4. **Agricolam spectō.**
5. **Spectō poētam.**
6. **Poētam spectō.**
7. **Ego spectō et nautam et agricolam.**
8. **Nauta nōn sum.**
9. **Agricolae sunt.**
10. **Poētae nōn estis.**

Answers on page 169.

LESSON 25

NEW WORD   **nautās**

MEANING   *sailors (direct object plural)*

When the direct object is plural the ending changes to **-ās**. So, **nautās** is the plural form of **nautam**.

What would be the direct object plural forms of **agricola** and **poēta**?

EXERCISES:

1. **Spectō nautās.**
2. **Nautās spectō.**
3. **Nōn spectō agricolās.**
4. **Agricolās spectō.**
5. **Ego spectō poētās.**
6. **Spectō nautam et agricolās.**
7. **Agricolam spectō.**
8. **Poēta es.**
9. **Nauta est.**
10. **Poētae sunt agricolae.**

Answers on page 169.

LESSON 26

NEW WORD   **stella**

MEANING   *star*

Think of the possible endings of **stella** and how each one would be used in a sentence.

EXERCISES:

1. **Stellam spectō.**
2. **Stellās nōn spectō.**
3. **Stellam ego spectō.**
4. **Ego spectō stellās.**
5. **Nautae sunt.**
6. **Nōn estis agricolae.**
7. **Poëtae sumus.**
8. **Spectō et agricolās et nautās.**
9. **Nauta nōn est poëta.**
10. **Agricola es.**

Answers on page 169.

LESSON 27

NEW WORD   **lūna**

MEANING   *moon*

Think of the possible endings of **lūna** and how each one would be used in a sentence.

EXERCISES:

1. **Lūnam spectō.**
2. **Spectō stellās.**
3. **Et lūnam et stellās spectō.**
4. **Spectō et stellās et lūnam.**
5. **Lūna nōn est stella.**
6. **Poēta est et agricola sum.**
7. **Spectō nautās.**
8. **Nōn estis agricolae.**
9. **Sumus poētae.**
10. **Agricolae sunt poētae.**

Answers on page 169.

LESSON 28

NEW WORD   **spectās**

MEANING   *you watch, you do watch, you are watching*

This chart should come in handy as we learn additional forms of **spectō**.

	SINGULAR	PLURAL
FIRST PERSON	**spectō**	
SECOND PERSON	**spectās**	
THIRD PERSON		

Remember: You must decide on your own whether to translate **spectās** as *you watch, you do watch,* or *you are watching.*

EXERCISES:

1. **Spectās lūnam.**
2. **Spectās stellās.**
3. **Et lūnam et stellās spectās.**
4. **Et nautās et agricolās spectās.**
5. **Ego spectō et nautās et agricolās.**
6. **Stellās ego nōn spectō.**
7. **Poētae nōn sumus.**
8. **Es agricola.**
9. **Agricolae nōn sunt.**
10. **Nauta nōn est poēta.**

Answers on page 169.

LESSON 29

NEW WORD   **spectat**

MEANING   *he/she/it watches, he/she/it does watch, he/she/it is watching*

The chart is getting fuller:

	SINGULAR	PLURAL
FIRST PERSON	**spectō**	
SECOND PERSON	**spectās**	
THIRD PERSON	**spectat**	

Do you remember the different ways to use **est**? **Spectat** is like that, too. Let's look at an example:

Nauta stellās spectat.

This sentence means *the sailor is watching the stars*. Here, it is clear that **nauta** is the subject of the sentence. Therefore, we leave out *he* and **spectat** simply means *is watching*.

Other times, there is no other word to be the subject of the sentence, as in the following example:

Stellās spectat.

This sentence means *he is watching the stars*. Here, there is no other word available to be the subject of the sentence. So, we translate **spectat** as *he is watching*.

Of course, **spectat** could also mean *she is watching* or *it is watching*. But for now, just translate **spectat** as *he is watching*.

41

EXERCISES:

1. **Spectat lūnam.**
2. **Nauta stellās spectat.**
3. **Spectat stellās et lūnam.**
4. **Agricola stellās nōn spectat.**
5. **Agricola nautam spectat.**
6. **Lūnam spectās.**
7. **Et poētam et agricolam spectō.**
8. **Agricolae nōn estis.**
9. **Agricola est.**
10. **Nautae sunt poētae.**

Answers on page 169.

LESSON 30

NEW WORD   **spectāmus**

MEANING   *we watch, we do watch, we are watching*

We're over halfway there!

	SINGULAR	PLURAL
FIRST PERSON	**spectō**	**spectāmus**
SECOND PERSON	**spectās**	
THIRD PERSON	**spectat**	

EXERCISES:

1. **Spectāmus agricolās.**
2. **Nōn spectāmus poētam.**
3. **Stellās spectat.**
4. **Et lūnam et stellās spectās.**
5. **Nautae nōn sunt.**
6. **Ego nōn spectō lūnam.**
7. **Agricola es et nauta sum.**
8. **Poēta est agricola.**
9. **Nōn es nauta.**
10. **Poētae sumus.**

Answers on page 170.

LESSON 31

NEW WORD   **spectātis**

MEANING   *y'all watch, y'all do watch, y'all are watching*

	SINGULAR	PLURAL
FIRST PERSON	**spectō**	**spectāmus**
SECOND PERSON	**spectās**	**spectātis**
THIRD PERSON	**spectat**	

EXERCISES:

1. **Spectātis stellam.**
2. **Agricolās spectātis.**
3. **Nautās spectātis.**
4. **Lūnam spectāmus.**
5. **Agricola poētam spectat.**
6. **Et lūnam et stellās spectās.**
7. **Nautās nōn spectat.**
8. **Sumus agricolae.**
9. **Nōn estis nautae.**
10. **Agricola est.**

Answers on page 170.

LESSON 32

NEW WORD   **spectant**

MEANING   *they watch, they do watch, they are watching*

The chart is now full!

	SINGULAR	PLURAL
FIRST PERSON	**spectō**	**spectāmus**
SECOND PERSON	**spectās**	**spectātis**
THIRD PERSON	**spectat**	**spectant**

Do you remember the different ways to use **sunt**? **Spectant** is like that, too. Let's look at an example:

Agricolae lūnam spectant.

This sentence means *the farmers are watching the moon*. Here, it is clear that **agricolae** is the subject of the sentence. Therefore, we leave out *they* and **spectant** simply means *are watching*.

Other times, there is no other word to be the subject of the sentence, as in the following example:

Stellās spectant.

This sentence means *they are watching the stars*. Here, there is no other word available to be the subject of the sentence. So, we translate **spectant** as *they are watching*.

EXERCISES:

1. **Poētās spectant.**
2. **Poētae stellās spectant.**
3. **Nautae et lūnam et stellās spectant.**
4. **Spectās agricolam.**
5. **Lūnam ego spectō.**
6. **Spectātis nautam.**
7. **Agricolae sunt.**
8. **Nōn sum nauta.**
9. **Agricola es.**
10. **Agricola est poēta.**

Answers on page 170.

LESSON 33

We now know all six present tense forms of **sum** and **spectō**. Let's review them now. Here is the chart for **sum:**

	SINGULAR	PLURAL
FIRST PERSON	**sum**	**sumus**
SECOND PERSON	**es**	**estis**
THIRD PERSON	**est**	**sunt**

Say all six forms in sequence: **sum, es, est, sumus, estis, sunt.** It is best to memorize them. Try to think of what each word means as you say it.

Here is the chart for **spectō:**

	SINGULAR	PLURAL
FIRST PERSON	**spectō**	**spectāmus**
SECOND PERSON	**spectās**	**spectātis**
THIRD PERSON	**spectat**	**spectant**

Repeat after me! **Spectō, spectās, spectat, spectāmus, spectātis, spectant.** Again, think of what each word means as you say it. Soon these groups of verbs will become second nature.

47

By now, you may be noticing a pattern to the endings of the verbs. If we made a chart of just the endings of **spectō** it would look like this:

	SINGULAR	PLURAL
FIRST PERSON	**-o**	**-mus**
SECOND PERSON	**-s**	**-tis**
THIRD PERSON	**-t**	**-nt**

As with the verbs themselves, it is best to memorize these endings so you can recognize them easily. Spell them out by letters: **-o**, **-s**, **-t**, **-mus**, **-tis**, **-nt**. From now on, when you learn a verb, you will know how to use it in all six present tense forms. You've come a long way from lesson 1. Keep up the good work!

LATIN EXPRESSIONS

Have you ever been told that something is a **non sequitur**?

Nōn, as you already know, means *not*. **Sequitur** means *it follows*. So literally, **non sequitur** means *it does not follow*. You may ask, "What doesn't follow?" That's a good question!

A **non sequitur** is when the conclusion drawn from the facts presented is not logically supported by the facts. Here's an example of a **non sequitur**:

- Fact #1: Spinach has lots of vitamins and minerals.
- Fact #2: Spinach is green.
- Conclusion: All green foods have lots of vitamins and minerals.

This conclusion is a **non sequitur** because *it does not follow* logically from what came before it. Fact #1 and fact #2 are both true, but the conclusion based on those facts is indeed faulty. Not all green foods have lots of vitamins and minerals. Green candy and green birthday cake may be delicious, but probably not very nutritious.

A **non sequitur** is an example of a logical fallacy, or mistake. Here are a few examples of some other common fallacies:

MERE ASSERTION Just because you say something is true does not prove that it is true.

APPEALING TO THE MASSES Just because a large number of people believes something is true does not prove that it is true.

AD HOMINEM This is another Latin expression that literally means *toward the man*. An **ad hominem** attack is an attempt to make someone seem untrustworthy by pointing out that person's flaws. This tactic is sometimes used as a last resort by those who are in danger of losing an argument. Even if you are successful in making your opponent look bad or untrustworthy, that still does not disprove his/her point.

LESSON 34

NEW WORD   **saepe**

MEANING   *often*

PRONUNCIATION TIP: The *ae* in **saepe** will sound different depending on which pronunciation style you adopt. In classical pronunciation, the *ae* in **saepe** sounds like the English word *eye*. In ecclesiastical pronunciation, it will sound like the *e* in *bet*.

Saepe is your first Latin adverb. An adverb is a word that describes how the action is taking place. When you translate the exercises, try to put the adverb where it sounds the best.

EXERCISES:

1. **Stellās saepe spectō.**
2. **Stellās saepe spectant.**
3. **Poētam saepe spectās.**
4. **Poēta est.**
5. **Agricolae estis.**
6. **Poēta nōn est agricola.**
7. **Et lūnam et stellās saepe spectāmus.**
8. **Agricolae sunt poētae.**
9. **Sumus poētae.**
10. **Lūnam saepe nōn spectātis.**

Answers on page 170.

LESSON 35

NEW WORD   **numerō**

MEANING   *I count, I do count, I am counting*

PRONUNCIATION TIP: If you are using the ecclesiastical style of pronunciation, remember to roll the *r* in **numerō** lightly.

The endings for **numerō** are the same as for **spectō**. Review them as often as you need to with this handy chart:

	SINGULAR	PLURAL
FIRST PERSON	**numerō**	**numerāmus**
SECOND PERSON	**numerās**	**numerātis**
THIRD PERSON	**numerat**	**numerant**

EXERCISES:

1. **Stellās numerō.**
2. **Numerās stellās.**
3. **Nauta stellās numerat.**
4. **Stellās saepe numerāmus.**
5. **Nautās numerātis.**
6. **Nautae stellās saepe numerant.**
7. **Agricolae nōn sunt poētae.**
8. **Nautae sunt.**
9. **Sumus agricolae.**
10. **Poēta es.**

Answers on page 170.

LESSON 36

NEW WORD   **pecūnia**

MEANING   *money*

When translating a Latin sentence, the first thing you should do is find the verb. Determine if the verb is singular or plural. Also, decide whether it is first person, second person, or third person. This will help you to determine the subject of the sentence more easily. Latin verbs are just packed with useful information!

EXERCISES:

1. **Pecūniam numerō.**
2. **Pecūniam saepe numerāmus.**
3. **Lūnam spectant.**
4. **Numerātis pecūniam.**
5. **Ego sum agricola.**
6. **Nautae stellās saepe numerant.**
7. **Agricola pecūniam numerat.**
8. **Poētae estis.**
9. **Nauta nōn est agricola.**
10. **Pecūniam saepe numerās.**

Answers on page 170.

LESSON 37

NEW WORD   **portō**

MEANING   *I carry, I do carry, I am carrying*

Review the endings of **portō** with this handy chart.

	SINGULAR	PLURAL
FIRST PERSON	**portō**	**portāmus**
SECOND PERSON	**portās**	**portātis**
THIRD PERSON	**portat**	**portant**

As you translate the exercises, remember to find the verb first.

EXERCISES:

1. **Pecūniam portō.**
2. **Portāmus pecūniam.**
3. **Et nautae et agricolae pecūniam portant.**
4. **Pecūniam saepe portat.**
5. **Nōn estis poētae.**
6. **Pecūniam portātis.**
7. **Pecūniam saepe portās.**
8. **Stellās numerās.**
9. **Agricolae sunt.**
10. **Nauta est.**

Answers on page 171.

LESSON 38

NEW WORD   **fēmina**

MEANING   *woman*

Fēmina is the first word we have encountered in this book that refers to someone of the female gender. Remember that **est** can be translated as *he is, she is,* or *it is.* Now, you will have an opportunity to translate sentences such as the following example:

> **Fēmina est.**

This sentence means *she is a woman.* It should be clear when to use *he, she,* or *it* in your translations.

When **est** does not refer directly to a female, continue to translate it as *he is.*

EXERCISES:

1. **Fēmina est.**
2. **Fēminae sumus.**
3. **Sum fēmina.**
4. **Fēmina pecūniam portat.**
5. **Pecūniam nōn portant.**
6. **Agricola est.**
7. **Ego pecūniam saepe nōn numerō.**
8. **Agricola es.**
9. **Nautae sunt poētae.**
10. **Lūnam spectāmus.**

Answers on page 171.

LATIN EXPRESSIONS

Have you ever heard the phrase **carpe diem** ?

Carpe is a verb in the form of a command. It is related to the word **carpo**. **Carpo** is a verb that can mean *pluck* or *snatch*, but can also mean *enjoy* or *make use of*. **Diem** is the direct object form of the word **dies** (pronounced *DEE-ace*), which means *day*. So literally, **carpe diem** is a command to *pluck the day*. **Carpe diem** is only part of what is perhaps the most famous line of poetry written in the Latin language. The entire line reads *pluck the day, entrusting as little as possible to the future*. This is the poet's way of encouraging the reader to take advantage of the moment and avoid procrastination. **Carpe diem** is usually expressed in English as *seize the day*.

In any language, poetry is filled with imagery and word choices that enrich the poem and add to its enjoyment. In this case, the use of the word **carpe** might bring to mind the imagery of plucking a flower from its stem. Or, because the word **carpe** can also mean *enjoy*, the author of the poem may have intended for both meanings to be present in the mind of the reader.

These words were penned by one of the greatest Roman poets, Quintus Horatius Flaccus (65–8 B.C.), commonly known as Horace. If you continue to study Latin, you may run into Horace again someday!

By the way, the word *procrastinate* is interesting because it comes from Latin root words. **Pro** means *for* and **crastinus** means *tomorrow*. If you put **pro** and **crastinus** together, what do you get? I'll tell you one of these days, when I get around to it.

And one last thing: Never put off your Latin homework until tomorrow. You'll never learn anything that way!

LESSON 39

NEW WORD   **semper**

MEANING   *always*

Semper is another adverb just like **saepe**.

EXERCISES:

1. **Pecūniam semper portō.**
2. **Semper portās pecūniam.**
3. **Nautae et lūnam et stellās semper spectant.**
4. **Fēmina pecūniam saepe numerat.**
5. **Nōn es agricola.**
6. **Fēminae sunt.**
7. **Pecūniam semper portātis.**
8. **Fēmina est.**
9. **Estis nautae.**
10. **Stellās saepe spectāmus.**

Answers on page 171.

LESSON 40

NEW WORD   **tabula**

MEANING   *writing tablet*

EXERCISES:

1. **Tabulam portō.**
2. **Tabulās portās.**
3. **Poētae tabulās semper portant.**
4. **Fēminae pecūniam saepe portant.**
5. **Lūna nōn est stella.**
6. **Pecūniam numerāmus.**
7. **Et stellās et lūnam spectātis.**
8. **Estis fēminae.**
9. **Fēmina pecūniam spectat.**
10. **Es fēmina.**

Answers on page 171.

LESSON 41

NEW WORD   **aqua**

MEANING   *water*

EXERCISES:

1. **Aquam ego portō.**
2. **Fēminae aquam portant.**
3. **Poēta tabulam saepe portat.**
4. **Aquam nōn portant.**
5. **Pecūniam numerātis.**
6. **Nautae aquam saepe spectant.**
7. **Pecūniam semper numerāmus.**
8. **Poētae nōn sumus.**
9. **Nautae sunt.**
10. **Agricola nōn es.**

Answers on page 171.

LESSON 42

NEW WORD   **puella**

MEANING   *puella*

EXERCISES:

1. **Puellae estis.**
2. **Puellae pecūniam numerant.**
3. **Puellās numerāmus.**
4. **Poētae nōn sunt.**
5. **Puellae stellās saepe numerant.**
6. **Poēta tabulās semper portat.**
7. **Sum fēmina.**
8. **Spectātis agricolās.**
9. **Puella aquam portat.**
10. **Lūnam spectās.**

Answers on page 171.

LESSON 43

NEW WORD   **amō**

MEANING   *I love, I do love, I am loving*
                  I like, I do like, I am liking

You must decide on your own whether to translate **amō** as *I love* or *I like*. How will you know which one to choose? Just use the one that sounds best in the context of the sentence.

Can you name the six forms of **amō** and tell what they mean?

EXERCISES:

1. **Fēminae agricolam nōn amant.**
2. **Puella nautam amat.**
3. **Poētam amāmus.**
4. **Et lūnam et stellās amō.**
5. **Puella aquam saepe portat.**
6. **Sum puella.**
7. **Pecūniam semper portātis.**
8. **Fēminae sumus et puellae sunt.**
9. **Nōn sum nauta.**
10. **Stellās numerāmus.**

Answers on page 172.

LESSON 44

NEW WORD   **silva**

MEANING   *forest*

PRONUNCIATION TIP: In classical pronunciation, the *v* in **silva** sounds like the *w* in *water*. In ecclesiastical pronunciation, it will sound like like the *v* in *violin*.

EXERCISES:

1. **Amō silvam.**
2. **Puellae silvam amant.**
3. **Nauta silvam nōn amat.**
4. **Silvam amātis.**
5. **Nautae sumus et agricolae estis.**
6. **Tabulās semper portāmus.**
7. **Ego aquam saepe portō.**
8. **Puella nautās spectat.**
9. **Lūnam spectāmus.**
10. **Agricola est poēta.**

Answers on page 172.

LESSON 45

NEW WORD   **scapha**

MEANING   *boat*

EXERCISES:

1. **Nauta scaphās amat.**
2. **Scaphās amās.**
3. **Puella et scaphās et nautās spectat.**
4. **Nautae scaphās saepe numerant.**
5. **Stellās numerātis.**
6. **Fēmina es.**
7. **Scapha nautās portat.**
8. **Puellae sunt.**
9. **Silvam amātis.**
10. **Aquam nōn portāmus.**

Answers on page 172.

LATIN EXPRESSIONS

What do the expressions **semper fidelis** and **semper paratus** mean?

Semper, as you already know, means *always*. **Fidelis** is an adjective that means *faithful*. So, **semper fidelis** simply means *always faithful*. **Semper Fidelis** is the motto of the United States Marine Corps. Sometimes this motto is seen in the abbreviated form **Semper Fi**.

Paratus means *prepared*. So, **semper paratus** means *always prepared*. **Semper Paratus** is the motto of the United States Coast Guard.

LESSON 46

NEW WORD **numquam**

MEANING *never*

Numquam is another adverb just like **saepe** and **semper**.

EXERCISES:

1. **Aquam numquam portō.**
2. **Fēmina tabulās numquam portat.**
3. **Nautae scaphās semper spectant.**
4. **Ego pecūniam semper numerō.**
5. **Spectās numquam lūnam.**
6. **Stellās saepe spectātis.**
7. **Puella silvam amat.**
8. **Poētae estis.**
9. **Nautae sumus et scaphās amāmus.**
10. **Nōn sum nauta.**

Answers on page 172.

LESSON 47

NEW WORD   **terra**

MEANING   *earth, land, soil*

Terra can mean *earth*, *land*, or *soil*. In this book, most of the time we will translate **terra** as *soil*.

EXERCISES:

1. **Agricola sum et terram amō.**
2. **Agricolae terram amant.**
3. **Nauta agricolam nōn amat.**
4. **Nauta scaphās amat.**
5. **Silvam amant.**
6. **Et lūnam et stellās spectātis.**
7. **Agricola nōn est.**
8. **Tabulam numquam portās.**
9. **Pecūniam saepe numerās.**
10. **Puella es.**

Answers on page 172.

LESSON 48

NEW WORD **sed**

MEANING *but*

The word **sed** often divides a sentence into two parts. To make translation easier, translate the part that comes before **sed** first and then translate the part that comes after **sed**.

EXERCISES:

1. **Agricola sum sed scaphās amō.**
2. **Fēmina pecūniam portat sed puellae aquam portant.**
3. **Nauta sum sed scaphās nōn amō.**
4. **Agricola est poēta.**
5. **Agricola silvam nōn amat.**
6. **Scaphās spectant.**
7. **Puellae aquam numquam portant.**
8. **Nauta silvam amat.**
9. **Stellās numerāmus.**
10. **Agricola nōn es.**

Answers on page 172.

LESSON 49

NEW WORD   **arō**

MEANING   *I plow, I do plow, I am plowing*

EXERCISES:

1. **Terram arō.**
2. **Agricolae terram arant.**
3. **Puella terram saepe arat.**
4. **Terram numquam arās.**
5. **Nautae scaphās amant.**
6. **Sumus agricolae sed scaphās amāmus.**
7. **Poēta nōn es sed tabulās saepe portās.**
8. **Agricolae estis sed terram numquam arātis.**
9. **Nautae sunt sed sumus poētae.**
10. **Poētae tabulās semper portant.**

Answers on page 173.

LESSON 50

NEW WORD   **ambulō**

MEANING   *I walk, I do walk, I am walking*

EXERCISES:

1. **Ambulāmus.**
2. **Fēmina ambulat.**
3. **Nautae pecūniam portant.**
4. **Terram saepe nōn arātis.**
5. **Nautae pecūniam saepe numerant.**
6. **Lūnam ego spectō sed stellās spectās.**
7. **Nauta es sed poēta sum.**
8. **Tabulās nōn portāmus.**
9. **Fēminae silvam amant.**
10. **Nautae sunt sed scaphās nōn amant.**

Answers on page 173.

LESSON 51

NEW WORD   **ad**

MEANING   *to, toward*

A preposition is a word that shows a relationship between two nouns. Examples of prepositions are *in, to, beside, with, behind, under,* and *over.* **Ad** is your first Latin preposition. **Ad** can mean *to* or *toward.* Use the meaning that makes the most sense in context.

When you use **ad**, the word it refers to must have the direct object ending. For instance, *to the forest* would be **ad silvam,** not **ad silva**. And in the plural, *toward the sailors* would be **ad nautās,** not **ad nautae.**

EXERCISES:

1. **Ad silvam ambulō.**
2. **Nautae ad scaphās ambulant.**
3. **Ad silvam ambulās sed ad aquam ambulō.**
4. **Pecūniam ad scapham portāmus.**
5. **Scapham ad aquam portant.**
6. **Agricola terram semper arat.**
7. **Ad silvam numquam ambulās.**
8. **Terram amō sed nōn sum agricola.**
9. **Poētae sunt sed tabulās numquam portant.**
10. **Fēmina nōn sum.**

Answers on page 173.

LESSON 52

NEW WORD   **acta**

MEANING   *seashore*

EXERCISES:

1. **Ad actam ego ambulō.**
2. **Ad actam nauta ambulat.**
3. **Actam amō.**
4. **Ambulāmus ad actam.**
5. **Puellae ad silvam saepe ambulant.**
6. **Nauta es sed scaphās nōn amās.**
7. **Nōn estis agricolae sed terram saepe arātis.**
8. **Tabulam saepe portās.**
9. **Puella ad actam ambulat.**
10. **Nōn est poēta.**

Answers on page 173.

LESSON 53

NEW WORD   **casa**

MEANING   *house*

EXERCISES:

1. **Ad casam ambulāmus.**
2. **Agricola ad casās aquam portat.**
3. **Ad casam ambulant.**
4. **Et actam et silvam amāmus.**
5. **Poētae sumus sed tabulās nōn portāmus.**
6. **Agricolae terram arant.**
7. **Poētae sunt.**
8. **Nōn es nauta.**
9. **Nautae sunt poētae.**
10. **Ad actam ambulant.**

Answers on page 173.

LATIN EXPRESSIONS

Occasionally the term **ad hoc** is used in a political or governmental context. What does it mean?

You already know that the word **ad** means *to* or *toward*. However, **ad** can have other meanings as well. In this case **ad** means *for the purpose of*. **Hoc** means *this*. So literally, **ad hoc** means *for the purpose of this* (*for this purpose*). Here is an example of how **ad hoc** is used:

> The mayor of Smithville got so many complaints about the traffic problems on Main Street that he appointed a special **ad hoc** committee to look into the problem.

The committee was created for the sole purpose of investigating and solving the traffic problem. It was created only *for this purpose.*

70

L E S S O N 5 4

CASES

In Latin, the endings of nouns change according to what role or function they play in a given sentence. Any noun may have many different forms. These different forms of nouns are called *cases*. When we use a noun as the subject of a sentence, that noun is said to be in the nominative case. We also use the nominative case for predicate nominatives. When we use a noun as a direct object, that noun is said to be in the accusative case. We also use the accusative case with certain prepositions like **ad**. There are five cases in all. Examine the chart below.

	SINGULAR	PLURAL
NOMINATIVE (SUBJECT/PREDICATE NOM.)	**nauta**	**nautae**
ACCUSATIVE (DIRECT OBJECT/OBJECT OF PREP.)	**nautam**	**nautās**

Each case performs certain functions while working together with the other cases to create meaningful sentences. As you can see from the chart, you already have experience with two of the five cases. As you learn the second, third, and fifth cases, you will be able to translate more complex (and interesting) exercises.

LESSON 55

NEW WORD   **nāvigō**

MEANING   *I sail, I do sail, I am sailing*

PRONUNCIATION TIP: In classical pronunciation, the *v* in **nāvigō** sounds like the *w* in *water*. In ecclesiastical pronunciation, it will sound like the *v* in *violin*.

EXERCISES:

1. **Saepe nāvigō.**
2. **Poēta numquam nāvigat.**
3. **Nautae nāvigant.**
4. **Ad casam ambulātis.**
5. **Ad actam nōn ambulāmus.**
6. **Nāvigātis sed ambulāmus.**
7. **Nautae estis sed sumus poētae.**
8. **Puella silvam amat.**
9. **Nōn amō scaphās et nōn amō aquam.**
10. **Nauta es sed numquam nāvigās.**

Answers on page 173.

LESSON 56

NEW WORD   **īnsula**

MEANING   *island*

EXERCISES:

1. **Ad īnsulam nāvigō.**
2. **Ad īnsulam saepe nāvigant.**
3. **Nautae ad īnsulās saepe nāvigant.**
4. **Fēmina īnsulās amat sed scaphās nōn amat.**
5. **Ad īnsulam saepe nōn nāvigās.**
6. **Scaphae ad īnsulam nāvigant.**
7. **Scapham ad actam portātis.**
8. **Nauta sum sed numquam nāvigō.**
9. **Agricola casam nōn amat.**
10. **Pecūniam numerant.**

Answers on page 174.

LESSON 57

NEW WORD   **circum**

MEANING   *around*

PRONUNCIATION TIP: In classical pronunciation, each *c* in **circum** sounds like the *k* in *kitchen*. In ecclesiastical pronunciation, the first *c* will sound like the *ch* in *cheese*, and the second one will sound like the *k* in *kitchen*.

Circum is another preposition. Like **ad**, **circum** takes the accusative (direct object) case.

EXERCISES:

1. **Circum īnsulam nāvigō.**
2. **Circum silvam saepe ambulāmus.**
3. **Nautae circum īnsulam semper nāvigant.**
4. **Ad casam ambulāmus.**
5. **Nōn sum agricola sed terram saepe arō.**
6. **Nōn es poēta sed tabulās semper portās.**
7. **Et stellās et lūnam saepe spectās.**
8. **Nauta scaphās amat.**
9. **Nōn sumus agricolae sed terram amāmus.**
10. **Et actam et silvam amō.**

Answers on page 174.

LESSON 58

NEW WORD   **natō**

MEANING   *I swim, I do swim, I am swimming*

EXERCISES:

1. **Ad īnsulam natō.**
2. **Nautae ad īnsulam natant.**
3. **Natās sed ambulō.**
4. **Aquam amō sed numquam natō.**
5. **Fēmina circum īnsulam saepe natat.**
6. **Nauta ad scapham natat.**
7. **Agricolae estis.**
8. **Circum īnsulās nāvigāmus.**
9. **Ad silvam semper ambulātis.**
10. **Puella scaphās amat sed nōn est nauta.**

Answers on page 174.

LESSON 59

NEW WORD   **prope**

MEANING   *near*

Prope is another preposition. Like **ad** and **circum**, **prope** takes the accusative (direct object) case.

EXERCISES:

1. **Prope actam ambulant.**
2. **Casa nōn est prope silvam.**
3. **Prope īnsulās nāvigāmus.**
4. **Scaphae circum īnsulās numquam nāvigant.**
5. **Es prope silvam.**
6. **Scaphās semper ego spectō.**
7. **Fēminae et puellae prope silvam sunt.**
8. **Aquam portātis.**
9. **Prope īnsulam semper natāmus.**
10. **Nauta nōn est sed scaphās amat.**

Answers on page 174.

LESSON 60

NEW WORD   **patria**

MEANING   *homeland*

EXERCISES:

1. **Patriam amō.**
2. **Ad patriam nāvigāmus.**
3. **Nauta patriam amat.**
4. **Scapha nautās ad patriam portat.**
5. **Fēmina circum īnsulam natat.**
6. **Patria est īnsula.**
7. **Actam amās sed silvam amō.**
8. **Nautae stellās et lūnam spectant.**
9. **Nōn estis agricolae.**
10. **Casa est prope aquam.**

Answers on page 174.

LESSON 61

NEW WORD   dēsīderō

MEANING   *I long for, I do long for, I am longing for*
I want, I do want, I am wanting

Sometimes **dēsīderō** will mean *long for*, and sometimes it will mean *want*. Use the context of the sentence and your own judgment to decide on the best translation for **dēsīderō**.

EXERCISES:

1. **Patriam saepe dēsīderō.**
2. **Agricolae aquam dēsīderant.**
3. **Fēminae actam dēsīderant.**
4. **Puella ad actam natat.**
5. **Scaphae circum īnsulam nāvigant.**
6. **Agricola terram amat.**
7. **Nōn es poēta.**
8. **Pecūniam semper dēsīderātis.**
9. **Agricola tabulam numquam portat.**
10. **Prope īnsulam sumus.**

Answers on page 174.

LESSON 62

ABLATIVE CASE

The fifth case on our chart is called the ablative case. The ablative case can be used in many ways.

	SINGULAR	PLURAL
NOMINATIVE (SUBJECT/PREDICATE NOM.)	nauta	nautae
ACCUSATIVE (DIRECT OBJECT/OBJECT OF PREP.)	nautam	nautās
ABLATIVE (MANY USES)	nautā	

The ablative singular is spelled the same as the nominative singular. The only visible difference is that the ablative singular has a mark over its final letter. This mark is called a *macron*. This macron will help you to distinguish the ablative singular from the nominative singular.

In this book you will learn two different ways to use the ablative case.

LESSON 63

NEW WORD   **in**

MEANING   *in, on* (takes ablative case), *into* (takes accusative case)

So far, all the prepositions you know (**ad, circum, prope**) take the accusative case. Not all prepositions, however, take the accusative case. Some prepositions take the ablative case. The word for this lesson, **in**, takes either the accusative case or the ablative case depending on what it means. **In** can mean *in, on,* or *into*. When **in** means *into*, it takes the accusative case. When **in** means *in* or *on*, it takes the ablative case.

When you translate the exercises you will have to figure out whether to translate **in** as *in* or *on*. To learn more about how the word **in** is used, examine the following examples:

In casā sum.

Because **in** takes the ablative case here, that narrows our choices down to either *in* or *on*. Because of the context, the best translation for **in** is *in*. So, the sentence means *I am in the house*. Here is another example:

In īnsulā sum.

Because **in** takes the ablative case here, that again narrows our choices down to either *in* or *on*. Because of the context, the best translation for **in** is *on*. So, the sentence means *I am on the island*. Here is another example:

Agricola in casam ambulat.

Because **in** takes the accusative case here (and because of the context of the sentence), we know that the best meaning for **in** is *into*. So, the sentence means *the farmer is walking into the house*.

EXERCISES:

1. **Sum in casā.**
2. **Nauta in īnsulā est.**
3. **Nautae in scaphā nōn sunt.**
4. **In īnsulā sumus.**
5. **Agricola circum casam ambulat.**
6. **Ad īnsulam saepe nāvigāmus.**
7. **Fēmina in casā est sed agricola in silvam ambulat.**
8. **Patriam dēsīderāmus.**
9. **Puella prope īnsulam natat.**
10. **Nōn es poēta sed tabulās portās.**

Answers on page 175.

LATIN EXPRESSIONS

Have you ever seen **c.** or **ca.** before a date?

The abbreviations **c.** and **ca.** stand for **circa** (usually pronounced in English as *SUR-kuh*). **Circa** is a Latin preposition that means *around*. It is related to the word **circum** which you already know. Writers usually place this expression before a year to express an approximate date when the exact date cannot be known. Here is an example of how **circa** is used:

> The quilt that Aunt Martha bought at the garage sale turned out to be a valuable antique from **c.** 1860.

Historians and other scholars have many ways of dating historical events (sometimes with extreme accuracy), but often it is just impossible to know for sure the year something happened.

LESSON 64

ABLATIVE PLURAL

PRONUNCIATION TIP: In both classical and ecclesiastical pronunciation, the *i* in **nautīs** sounds like the *ee* in *meet* and *sweet*.

The ablative plural has the ending **-īs**. Compare the ablative plural to the forms you already know in the chart below:

	SINGULAR	PLURAL
NOMINATIVE (SUBJECT/PREDICATE NOM.)	nauta	nautae
ACCUSATIVE (DIRECT OBJECT/OBJECT OF PREP.)	nautam	nautās
ABLATIVE (MANY USES)	nautā	nautīs

EXERCISES:

1. **Agricolae in casīs sunt.**
2. **Nautae in scaphīs nōn sunt.**
3. **Nauta scapham in aquam portat.**
4. **Scaphae in aquā sunt.**
5. **Nauta in īnsulā est.**
6. **Nauta ad patriam nāvigat.**
7. **Nauta ego nōn sum sed scaphās amō.**
8. **Puellae ad actam semper ambulant.**
9. **Prope īnsulam saepe natātis.**
10. **Nauta scapham dēsīderat.**

Answers on page 175.

LESSON 65

NEW WORD   **schola**

MEANING   *school*

Review the noun endings you know with this handy chart:

	Singular	Plural
Nominative (subject/predicate nom.)	schola	scholae
Accusative (direct object/object of prep.)	scholam	scholās
Ablative (many uses)	scholā	scholīs

EXERCISES:

1. **Schola in silvā est.**
2. **Puellae ad scholam ambulant.**
3. **Puella est in scholā.**
4. **Puella tabulam ad scholam portat.**
5. **Nauta es sed scaphās nōn amās.**
6. **Nauta ego sum sed agricola es.**
7. **Ad īnsulās nāvigāmus sed patriam dēsīderāmus.**
8. **Agricolae sumus sed terram numquam arāmus.**
9. **Scapha in aquā est.**
10. **In scaphīs estis sed in aquā sum.**

Answers on page 175.

LESSON 66

EVEN MORE ABOUT EST AND SUNT

Early in this book you learned two ways to use **est** and **sunt**. You learned that if a sentence already has a subject, **est** just means *is*. But, if a sentence has no other word to be the subject, **est** means *he is, she is,* or *it is*.

Likewise, you learned that if a sentence already has a subject, **sunt** just means *are*. But, if a sentence has no other word to be the subject, **sunt** means *they are*.

Now I will show you another way that the words **est** and **sunt** are used in Latin. **Est** is used to mean *there is* and **sunt** is used to mean *there are*. Examine the following examples:

> **Est fēmina in scaphā** (*There is a woman in the boat*).
> **Sunt nautae in īnsulā** (*There are sailors on the island*).

Did you notice that in those examples **est** and **sunt** came first in the sentence? Keep this third possible use of **est** and **sunt** in mind as you do the exercises, especially when **est** or **sunt** is the first word of the sentence.

EXERCISES:

1. **Sunt puellae in casā.**
2. **Est scapha prope actam.**
3. **Prope īnsulam numquam natō.**
4. **Silvam dēsīderātis sed scaphās amāmus.**
5. **Īnsulās nōn amās.**
6. **Sunt et agricolae et fēminae in casīs.**
7. **Poēta terram et aquam amat.**
8. **Fēminae in silvīs saepe ambulant.**
9. **Est pecūnia in scaphā.**
10. **Nōn sum agricola sed terram amō.**

Answers on page 175.

LESSON 67

NEW WORD   **cotīdiē**

MEANING   *daily*

PRONUNCIATION TIP: **Cotīdiē** has four syllables. In classical pronunciation it will sound like *ko-TEE-di-ay*. In ecclesiastical pronunciation, the *e* at the end will sound like the *e* in *bet*.

Cotīdiē is another adverb like **saepe**, **semper**, and **numquam**.

EXERCISES:

1. **Ad actam cotīdiē ambulāmus.**
2. **Nautae circum īnsulam cotīdiē nāvigant.**
3. **Agricola terram cotīdiē arat.**
4. **Puellae ad scholam cotīdiē ambulant.**
5. **Aquam ad casās cotīdiē portāmus.**
6. **Sunt nautae in īnsulīs.**
7. **Estis poētae sed agricolae sumus.**
8. **Lūnam spectātis sed stellās spectāmus.**
9. **Patriam dēsīderās sed īnsulās dēsīderō.**
10. **Poēta in casam ambulat.**

Answers on page 175.

LESSON 68

NEW WORD   **ā, ab**

MEANING   *from* (takes the ablative case)

PRONUNCIATION TIP: In both classical and ecclesiastical pronunciation, the *a* in **ā** and **ab** sounds like the *o* in *not* and *pot*.

This preposition can be spelled either **ā** or **ab**. Generally speaking, **ā** is used if the next word starts with a consonant and **ab** is used if the next word starts with a vowel.

We have similar spelling variations in English, too. Consider the following examples:

> A book
> An apple

A and *an* are the same word but with one important difference: *a* comes before words that begin with a consonant and *an* comes before words that begin with a vowel. Why the variation in spelling? This is done in order to make pronunciation easier. For example, it is easier to say *a book* than *an book* and it is easier to say *an apple* than *a apple*.

Likewise, **ab īnsulā** is easier to say than **ā īnsulā** and **ā patriā** is easier than **ab patriā**. The concept is the same in Latin as it is in English.

EXERCISES:

1. **Puella ā casā ad scholam ambulat.**
2. **Scaphae ab īnsulā ad patriam cotīdiē nāvigant.**
3. **Fēmina pecūniam cotīdiē numerat.**
4. **Sunt agricolae in casā.**
5. **Ab īnsulā ad patriam nāvigāmus.**
6. **Nautae in īnsulā nōn sunt.**
7. **Ad actam cotīdiē ambulāmus.**

86

8. **Ego circum īnsulam nāvigō.**
9. **Estis agricolae sed terram numquam arātis.**
10. **Fēmina tabulās portat.**

Answers on page 175.

LESSON 69

NEW WORD   cum

MEANING   *with* (takes the ablative case)

EXERCISES:

1. **Fēmina est in casā cum puellīs.**
2. **Agricola cum nautīs nōn est.**
3. **Ambulō ad actam cum nautīs.**
4. **Fēminae in scaphā cum nautīs sunt.**
5. **Puellae ā scholā ad actam cotīdiē ambulant.**
6. **Agricola est.**
7. **Nautae sunt in scaphīs et in īnsulā.**
8. **Terram amō sed agricola nōn sum.**
9. **Puellae in scholam cum tabulīs ambulant.**
10. **In scaphā sum sed in aquā es.**

Answers on page 176.

LESSON 70

NEW WORD   **taberna**

MEANING   *shop*

EXERCISES:

1. **In tabernam ambulāmus.**
2. **Puellae ā scholā ad tabernam cotīdiē ambulant.**
3. **Pecūnia in scaphā est cum nautīs.**
4. **Patriam dēsīderō.**
5. **Sunt nautae in scaphīs.**
6. **Scapha circum īnsulam saepe nāvigat.**
7. **Nautae estis sed aquam nōn amātis.**
8. **In aquā numquam natās.**
9. **Poēta tabulās semper portat.**
10. **Prope silvam nōn sumus.**

Answers on page 176.

LESSON 71

NEW WORD   **sine**

MEANING   *without* (takes the ablative case)

EXERCISES:

1. **Fēmina ad tabernam sine pecūniā numquam ambulat.**
2. **Nautae in īnsulā sine scaphā sunt.**
3. **Nauta es.**
4. **Puellae in īnsulā sunt sed ego in scaphā sum.**
5. **Nauta in īnsulā est sed patriam dēsīderat.**
6. **Poēta ad actam cotīdiē ambulat.**
7. **Agricola patriam amat.**
8. **Ā scholā ad actam ambulāmus.**
9. **Terram numquam arātis sed ego cotīdiē terram arō.**
10. **Fēmina in silvam cum puellīs ambulat.**

Answers on page 176.

LATIN EXPRESSIONS

Every college student dreams of graduating **summa cum laude**. Others are pleased to graduate **magna cum laude**. Still others are satisfied to graduate **cum laude**. Some are happy just to graduate at all!

Let's work our way up from the bottom. **Cum**, as you already know, means *with*. **Laude** is the ablative singular form of the word **laus** which means *praise*. This is necessary because **cum** takes the ablative case. So literally, **cum laude** means *with praise*. This term is usually applied to graduates who have achieved a certain grade average during their college years.

Those with even better grades earn the designation **magna cum laude** at graduation. **Magna** is an adjective that means *great*. **Magna** goes with **laude**. So literally, **magna cum laude** means *with great praise*. Remember that in Latin, the words don't have to be in the right order. Even though **magna** and **laude** are separated by the word **cum** they still go together. Having the words in this order puts more emphasis on the word **magna**.

Summa cum laude is the highest honor of all. The word **summa** is an adjective that means *highest*. **Summa** goes with **laude**. So literally, **summa cum laude** means *with highest praise*.

Only one person in each graduating class can graduate **summa cum laude,** and that person is called the *valedictorian*. Incidentally, the word *valedictorian* comes from Latin roots. **Vale** means *good-bye*. **Dictus** is a form of the Latin word that means *to say*. So literally, the English word *valedictorian* means *one who says good-bye*. This is because the valedictorian usually gives the final speech at the graduation ceremony, wishing the graduates well as they go their separate ways.

The person who graduates second in a class is called the *salutatorian*. In Latin, **salutare** means *to greet*. So literally, the English word *salutatorian* means *one who greets*. This is because the salutatorian traditionally is the first to speak at the graduation ceremony.

LESSON 72

POSSESSION

Possessive words show ownership of something. In English, we often show possession by using an apostrophe followed by the letter *s*. Observe the following examples:

> Fred's car
> The nation's flag
> Arizona's capital

Sometimes we show possession by using the word *of*.

> The peak of the mountain
> The smell of garlic
> The beginning of the show

Therefore, in English, when you want to show possession of something, you must decide whether to use the letter *s* with an apostrophe, or the word *of*.

Here are a few of the most basic rules to remember when using apostrophes:

	RULE	EXAMPLE
RULE #1	To make a noun that does not end in *s* possessive, just add an apostrophe and an *s*.	Lauren always wants to borrow Kate's Latin book.
RULE #2	To make a singular noun that ends in *s* possessive, add an apostrophe and an *s* (just like rule #1).	The class's favorite subject was Latin.
RULE #3	To make a plural noun that ends in *s* possessive, add an apostrophe to the end of the word.	Due to increased interest in Latin, all the books' covers are starting to wear out.

LESSON 73

THE GENITIVE CASE

In Latin, the most common way to show possession is to use the second of the five cases, called the *genitive case*. As you study the chart below, notice that the genitive singular looks identical to the nominative plural.

	SINGULAR	PLURAL
NOMINATIVE (SUBJECT/PREDICATE NOM.)	**nauta**	**nautae**
GENITIVE (POSSESSION)	**nautae**	
ACCUSATIVE (DIRECT OBJECT/OBJECT OF PREP.)	**nautam**	**nautās**
ABLATIVE (MANY USES)	**nautā**	**nautīs**

How do we use the genitive case in Latin? Consider the following example:

Scapha nautae (*the sailor's boat*)

In this example the *boat* belongs to the *sailor*. *Sailor* (**nauta**) is in the genitive case (**nautae**) because the sailor possesses the boat. Usually the word in the genitive case comes immediately after the word it possesses. Here is another example:

Casa agricolae (*the farmer's house*)

In this example, the house belongs to the farmer. Farmer (**agricola**) is in the genitive case (**agricolae**) because the farmer is possessing the house.

Here is how a complete sentence might look with a genitive in it:

In scaphā nautae sum (*I am in the sailor's boat*).

Right now you may be concerned about confusing the nominative plural with the genitive singular. After all, they do look alike. But don't worry—since genitives usually follow the words they possess, they are usually easy to recognize.

Also, when you are translating from Latin to English you must use your best judgment in deciding whether to use an apostrophe and *s* or the word *of* to show possession. At first, you may want to try each one and see which one sounds better. The context of the sentence will help you provide the best translation.

EXERCISES:

1. **Pecūnia nautae**
2. **Casa agricolae**
3. **In scaphā nautae sumus.**
4. **Pecūniam agricolae portās.**
5. **Puella ad casam agricolae cotīdiē ambulat.**
6. **Scapham ā casā ad actam portāmus.**
7. **Īnsulās amāmus sed silvam amātis.**
8. **Poēta in casā cum agricolīs est.**
9. **Ad tabernam sine pecūniā numquam ambulāmus.**
10. **Nautae circum īnsulam nāvigant.**

Answers on page 176.

LESSON 74

NEW WORD   **nautārum**

MEANING   *of the sailors* (genitive plural)

The plural of the genitive case has the ending **-ārum**. This one is easy to remember because it does not look like any of the other endings.

	SINGULAR	PLURAL
NOMINATIVE (SUBJECT / PREDICATE NOM.)	**nauta**	**nautae**
GENITIVE (POSSESSION)	**nautae**	**nautārum**
ACCUSATIVE (DIRECT OBJECT / OBJECT OF PREP.)	**nautam**	**nautās**
ABLATIVE (MANY USES)	**nautā**	**nautīs**

We use this form to show that something is possessed by more that one person or thing. Consider the following example:

Scapha nautārum (*the sailors' boat*)

In this example, the boat is owned by more than one sailor. So, we use the genitive plural, **nautārum**. The English translation of **nautārum** is *sailors'*. Notice that the apostrophe here is after the letter *s*, not before. You may need to refer back to the basic apostrophe rules given in lesson 72.

EXERCISES:

1. **Patria nautārum**
2. **Schola puellārum**
3. **Tabulās poētārum portō.**

94

4. Fēminae et puellae in scaphā sunt cum nautīs.
5. Poēta stellās numerat.
6. Fēminae circum īnsulam in scaphīs nāvigant.
7. Pecūnia agricolae in silvā est.
8. Puella ā scholā ad tabernam ambulat.
9. Silvam amās sed puellae actam amant.
10. In aquā sine scaphā estis.

Answers on page 177.

LESSON 75

NEW WORD   **familia**

MEANING   *family*

EXERCISES:

1. Familia agricolae in casā est.
2. Familiae nautārum in īnsulā sunt.
3. Familia fēminae in silvā est.
4. Nautae ad patriam cum pecūniā saepe nāvigant.
5. Poēta es sed agricola sum.
6. In tabernam sine pecūniā numquam ambulō.
7. Ad īnsulam cotīdiē nāvigātis.
8. Prope īnsulam nōn estis.
9. In īnsulā sine scaphīs sumus.
10. Agricolae patriam dēsīderant.

Answers on page 177.

LESSON 76

NEW WORD   **fābula**

MEANING   *story*

EXERCISES:

1. Fābulās agricolae amō.
2. Puellae fābulam nautae nōn amant.
3. Agricola scaphās nautārum amat.
4. Puella est in scholā sed actam dēsīderat.
5. Nautae scapham ad aquam portant.
6. Familia agricolae ad tabernam ambulat.
7. Nautae in īnsulā sunt sine scaphīs et sine pecūniā.
8. Aquam numquam portās sed semper aquam portō.
9. Terram semper arāmus sed in casā semper estis.
10. Circum īnsulam nōn nāvigāmus.

Answers on page 177.

LESSON 77

NEW WORD   **incola**

MEANING   *inhabitant*

EXERCISES:

1. **Incola īnsulae es.**
2. **Sunt incolae in īnsulīs.**
3. **Incolae īnsulārum in aquā natant.**
4. **Nautae incolās īnsulae spectant.**
5. **Incolae silvae ad actam cotīdiē ambulant.**
6. **Incolae silvae fābulās amant.**
7. **Familia poētae patriam dēsīderat.**
8. **Puellae tabulās ad scholam cotīdiē portant.**
9. **Puellae in casam ambulant.**
10. **Cum nautīs ad īnsulam nāvigās.**

Answers on page 177.

LESSON 78

NEW WORD   **narrō**

MEANING   *I tell, I do tell, I am telling*

EXERCISES:

1. **Fābulam narrō.**
2. **Agricola fābulam narrat.**
3. **Nautae fābulās narrant.**
4. **Fābulās nautae amāmus.**
5. **Nautae sunt in īnsulā et fābulās narrant.**
6. **Incolae īnsulae prope actam natant.**
7. **Et agricola et poēta ad tabernam ambulant.**
8. **Scaphās amātis sed nautae nōn estis.**
9. **Scapha familiās nautārum ad īnsulam portat.**
10. **Scapha nautārum in aquā est.**

Answers on page 178.

LATIN EXPRESSIONS

Have you ever opened a book and seen a little label with the owner's name on it? If so, then you have probably seen the term **ex libris**.

Those little labels are called *bookplates*. A typical bookplate might say **ex libris John Smith**. **Ex** is a preposition that means *out of*. **Ex** takes the ablative case. **Libris** is the ablative plural form of the word **liber** which means *book*. So literally, **ex libris** means *out of the books*. A smoother way to express **ex libris** would be *from the library (of)*. Think of the person's name as being possessive. So, **ex libris John Smith** would mean something like *from the library of John Smith*.

LESSON 79

INDIRECT OBJECTS

You already know that a direct object is a noun that is the target of the action being performed by the subject of the sentence. An indirect object is a secondary target of the action done by the subject of the sentence. The indirect object is the party that is receiving or benefiting from the action being performed by the subject. Indirect objects are often accompanied by *to* or *for*. In each of the following examples, the indirect object is underlined:

> He gave the book to <u>Johnny</u>.
> She told a story to the <u>class</u>.
> She bought some presents for her <u>friends</u>.
> He showed his rock collection to <u>Mr. Green.</u>

And now, the same sentences but with a different word order:

> He gave <u>Johnny</u> the book.
> She told the <u>class</u> a story.
> She bought her <u>friends</u> some presents.
> He showed <u>Mr. Green</u> his rock collection.

So, although these two ways of expressing the indirect object are worded differently, they still mean the same thing.

By the way, take care not to confuse indirect objects with objects of the preposition. Consider the following example:

> I sailed to the island.

In this example the word *to* is just a preposition, not part of an indirect object.

In the following exercises, see if you can identify the direct object and the indirect object.

EXERCISES:

1. I loaned the money to my friend.
2. We donated money to the charity.
3. He showed the class an example.
4. Let's get some curtains for the house.
5. Henry got some seeds for the garden.
6. They made us some sandwiches.
7. He told the judge his story.
8. The band played another song for the audience.
9. I brought copies for everyone.
10. My mother bought me a shirt.

Answers on page 178.

LESSON 80

NEW WORD   **nautae**

MEANING   *to the sailor or for the sailor* (indirect object form)

For indirect objects we use the third case, which is called the *dative case*. **Nautae** is the dative singular form of **nauta**. Let's look at the chart again and review the forms we know so far:

	SINGULAR	PLURAL
NOMINATIVE (SUBJECT/PREDICATE NOM.)	**nauta**	**nautae**
GENITIVE (POSSESSION)	**nautae**	**nautārum**
DATIVE (INDIRECT OBJECT)	**nautae**	
ACCUSATIVE (DIRECT OBJECT/OBJECT OF PREP.)	**nautam**	**nautās**
ABLATIVE (MANY USES)	**nautā**	**nautīs**

Notice that the dative singular looks identical to the nominative plural and the genitive singular. As before, when you see a noun with the **-ae** ending you must use the context of the sentence to determine whether it is nominative plural, genitive singular, or dative singular.

Use the dative case for indirect objects the same way you would in English. Consider the following example:

Agricolae fābulam narrō *(I am telling the story to the farmer).*

In the exercises in this book, the indirect object will come before the direct object, as in the example shown above.

102

EXERCISES:

1. **Nautae fābulam narrō.**
2. **Poēta agricolae fābulam narrat.**
3. **Puellae poētae fābulās narrant.**
4. **Scapha nautae in aquā est.**
5. **Incolae īnsulārum in aquā saepe natant.**
6. **Schola puellārum in silvā nōn est.**
7. **Agricola es sed poēta sum.**
8. **Familia agricolae in casā est.**
9. **Patriam amō sed ad īnsulam nāvigō.**
10. **Incolae silvae sumus sed actam amāmus.**

Answers on page 178.

LESSON 81

NEW WORD   **nautīs**

MEANING   *to* or *for the sailors* (dative plural)

Nautīs is the plural of the dative case. Compare it with the other forms you know in the chart below.

	SINGULAR	PLURAL
NOMINATIVE (SUBJECT/PREDICATE NOM.)	**nauta**	**nautae**
GENITIVE (POSSESSION)	**nautae**	**nautārum**
DATIVE (INDIRECT OBJECT)	**nautae**	**nautīs**
ACCUSATIVE (DIRECT OBJECT/OBJECT OF PREP.)	**nautam**	**nautās**
ABLATIVE (MANY USES)	**nautā**	**nautīs**

As you have probably noticed, the dative plural looks identical to the ablative plural. When you see a word that ends in -**īs**, you must use the context to decide if it is dative plural or ablative plural.

You may be thinking to yourself, "Wouldn't the endings be easier to memorize and recognize if each ending were different from all the other endings?" This is a valid observation. If each ending were unique and different from every other ending, there would be no confusion among nominative plural, genitive singular, and dative singular (as well as between dative plural and ablative plural). However, with practice and experience you will be able to tell the difference easily.

EXERCISES:

1. **Nautīs fābulās narrāmus.**
2. **Nauta agricolīs fābulam narrat.**
3. **Poētae puellae fābulam narrant.**

104

4. **Fēminae in silvā sunt.**
5. **Incolae īnsulārum scaphās amant.**
6. **Poēta in tabernam sine pecūniā ambulat.**
7. **Pecūniam semper portās.**
8. **Nautae circum īnsulam in scaphīs nāvigant.**
9. **Puellae in scholā sunt sed et actam et silvam dēsīderant.**
10. **Terram semper arāmus sed in silvā semper estis.**

Answers on page 178.

LATIN EXPRESSIONS

Have you ever wondered what **per capita** means?

Per has several meanings. In this expression, **per** means *by*. **Capita** means *heads*. Literally, **per capita** means *by heads*. This term is used to show how something averages out on a person-by-person basis. Here's an example of how this term is used:

> Fructessa, a large island country, consumes more bananas yearly than any other country. However, the smaller country of Karpovia consumes more bananas yearly **per capita** than any other country.

You see, as a country, Fructessa may consume a higher total number of bananas simply because it has a greater number of people. But each individual resident of Karpovia eats more bananas on average than each individual resident of Fructessa.

LESSON 82

NEW WORD   **dō**

MEANING   *I give, I do give, I am giving*

This verb will provide us with more opportunities to practice using the dative case.

	SINGULAR	PLURAL
FIRST PERSON	**dō**	**dāmus**
SECOND PERSON	**dās**	**dātis**
THIRD PERSON	**dat**	**dant**

EXERCISES:

1. **Ego agricolae pecūniam dō.**
2. **Poēta puellīs tabulās dat.**
3. **Incolīs īnsulae aquam dāmus.**
4. **Fēmina puellīs tabulās dat.**
5. **Nautīs fābulās narrāmus.**
6. **Ā scaphā ad īnsulam natō.**
7. **In aquā scapha nautārum est.**
8. **Puellae fābulās semper amant.**
9. **Estis fēminae.**
10. **Terram saepe arātis.**

Answers on page 179.

LESSON 83

REVIEW

Now you know the endings for all five cases, both singular and plural. Review them with the chart below:

	SINGULAR	PLURAL
NOMINATIVE (SUBJECT/PREDICATE NOM.)	**-a**	**-ae**
GENITIVE (POSSESSION)	**-ae**	**-ārum**
DATIVE (INDIRECT OBJECT)	**-ae**	**-īs**
ACCUSATIVE (DIRECT OBJECT/OBJECT OF PREP.)	**-am**	**-ās**
ABLATIVE (MANY USES)	**-ā**	**-īs**

By now you probably have chanted the verbs and verb endings many times. In the same way, you should chant and memorize these noun endings. If you memorize the chart displayed below, your reading and comprehension skills will improve.

	SINGULAR	PLURAL
NOMINATIVE (SUBJECT/PREDICATE NOM.)	**nauta**	**nautae**
GENITIVE (POSSESSION)	**nautae**	**nautārum**
DATIVE (INDIRECT OBJECT)	**nautae**	**nautīs**
ACCUSATIVE (DIRECT OBJECT/OBJECT OF PREP.)	**nautam**	**nautās**
ABLATIVE (MANY USES)	**nautā**	**nautīs**

A set of noun endings like this is called a declension (*deh-KLEN-shun*). A few lessons from now, you will learn more about declensions and how they figure into Latin grammar.

LESSON 84

NEW WORD   **-que** ending

MEANING   *and*

You already know that **et** means *and*. But there is another way to express the word *and* in Latin. If you add **-que** to the end of a word, it puts *and* between that word and the word that came before it. For example:

> **Nauta agricolaque** (*the sailor and the farmer*)
> **Aqua terraque** (*the water and the soil*)
> **Lūnam stellāsque spectō** (*I am watching the moon and the stars*).

EXERCISES:

1. **Actam silvamque amō.**
2. **Fēminae puellaeque ad actam ambulant.**
3. **Pecūniam tabulāsque saepe portātis.**
4. **Stellās lūnamque spectō.**
5. **Poēta nautīs fābulam narrat.**
6. **Prope patriam nōn sumus.**
7. **Ad actam saepe nōn ambulāmus.**
8. **Ad scholam cum puellīs cotīdiē ambulāmus.**
9. **Nauta patriam amat sed ad īnsulās navigat.**
10. **Pecūniam poētae semper dās.**

Answers on page 179.

LESSON 85

NEW WORD   **aedificō**

MEANING   *I build, I do build, I am building*

EXERCISES:

1. **Agricola casam aedificat.**
2. **Casam scaphamque ego aedificō.**
3. **Casam in īnsulā aedificātis.**
4. **Poēta nautīs pecūniam dat.**
5. **Puellae tabulās ad scholam semper portant.**
6. **Fēmina in casā est sed agricola in silvā est.**
7. **Nauta es sed aquam nōn amās.**
8. **Prope actam casās aedificāmus.**
9. **Scapha nautārum est in īnsulā.**
10. **Agricolae estis.**

Answers on page 179.

LESSON 86

NEW WORD   **servō**

MEANING   *I guard, I do guard, I am guarding*

EXERCISES:

1. **Casās servō.**
2. **Nautae īnsulam scaphāsque servant.**
3. **Casam agricolae servāmus.**
4. **Casās scaphāsque aedificātis.**
5. **Scapha ad īnsulam sine nautīs nāvigat.**
6. **Sine pecūniā poēta ad tabernam ambulat.**
7. **Scaphae nautās ab īnsulā ad actam portant.**
8. **Puellīs fābulās narrātis sed casam aedificō.**
9. **Agricolae nautae aquam dant.**
10. **Casa prope silvam nōn est.**

Answers on page 179.

LESSON 87

NEW WORD   **labōrō**

MEANING   *I work, I do work, I am working*

EXERCISES:

1. **In casā labōrō.**
2. **Fēminae puellaeque in silvā labōrant.**
3. **Aquam ego portō sed nōn labōrātis.**
4. **Labōrāmus sed in aquā natātis.**
5. **Puella cum agricolīs labōrat.**
6. **Patriam dēsīderās.**
7. **Poētīs pecūniam numquam dāmus.**
8. **Es in aquā sed in scaphā sum.**
9. **Casam aedificō.**
10. **Nauta in casā agricolae nōn est.**

Answers on page 180.

LESSON 88

INFINITIVES

An infinitive is the word *to* plus a verb. Here are some examples of infinitives:

> to walk
> to eat
> to run
> to be

Let's examine some of the different ways infinitives are used:

> I like to sing.
> I want to be a teacher.
> To eat a watermelon is sheer delight.
> I am unable to finish my homework.
> I want to play checkers.

Try to locate the infinitive in each of the exercises below. But be careful! A few of the exercises do not have infinitives. Can you tell which ones they are?

EXERCISES:

1. I do not like to wash the dishes.
2. They want to play a different game.
3. I went to the store.
4. Charles wants to be a policeman.
5. To forgive is divine.
6. She wants to return that sweater to the store.
7. Jenny would like to play the clarinet.
8. We will not go to the party.
9. She will go to the furniture store to buy a chair.
10. Throw the ball to Jeremy.

Answers on page 180.

LESSON 89

NEW WORD   **spectāre**

MEANING   *to watch*

In English, it takes two words to express an infinitive: the word *to* and a verb. In Latin, it only takes one word to express an infinitive. Examine the ending of the word **spectāre**. Instead of having **-ō** as the ending, it ends in **-āre**. Let's use **spectāre** in a sentence:

Stellās spectāre amō (*I love to watch the stars*).

To find the infinitive form of each of the verbs you know so far, simply remove the **-ō** from the end of the word and add **-āre**. Here are a few examples using verbs you already know:

numerō becomes **numerāre** (*to count*)
portō becomes **portāre** (*to carry*)
arō becomes **arāre** (*to plow*)
ambulō becomes **ambulāre** (*to walk*)
nāvigō becomes **nāvigāre** (*to sail*)
natō becomes **natāre** (*to swim*)

EXERCISES:
1. **Scaphās spectāre amō.**
2. **Terram arāre nōn amō.**
3. **Puellae ad scholam ambulāre nōn dēsīderant.**
4. **Nautae ad īnsulās nāvigāre amant.**
5. **Puellae in silvam ambulāre dēsīderant.**
6. **Casās prope actam aedificāre dēsīderāmus.**
7. **Nauta agricolīs fābulās narrat.**
8. **In casā agricolārum labōrāmus.**
9. **Puellīs pecūniam dō.**
10. **Casās scaphāsque servāmus.**

Answers on page 180.

LESSON 90

NEW WORD   **possum**

MEANING   *I am able*

Examine the last three letters of the word **possum**. Do they look familiar? **Possum** is just the word **sum** with the prefix **pos-** added to the beginning of the word.

Possum cannot do anything by itself. It needs an infinitive to complete its meaning. Consider the following examples:

> **Aquam portāre possum** *(I am able to carry the water).*
> **Ad īnsulam nāvigāre possum** *(I am able to sail to the island).*
> **Stellās numerāre nōn possum** *(I am not able to count the stars).*

In each of these examples, **possum** works with an infinitive to show what activity the subject of the sentence is or is not able to do.

EXERCISES:

1. **Natāre possum.**
2. **Scapham portāre nōn possum.**
3. **Ad īnsulam nāvigāre possum.**
4. **Ego ad īnsulam ambulāre nōn possum.**
5. **In silvā natāre nōn possum.**
6. **Incolae silvārum casās servant.**
7. **Ad patriam nāvigāre dēsīderāmus.**
8. **Poēta puellīs fābulās narrāre amat.**
9. **Pecūniam cotīdiē numerāre amō.**
10. **Pecūnia nautae in scaphā est.**

Answers on page 180.

L E S S O N 91

Here are all the present tense forms of **possum**. Notice that these forms are very easy to recognize because they are simply **sum**, **es**, **est**, **sumus**, **estis** and **sunt** with a prefix of either **pos-** or **pot-** added to the beginning of the word.

	SINGULAR	PLURAL
FIRST PERSON	**possum**	**possumus**
SECOND PERSON	**potes**	**potestis**
THIRD PERSON	**potest**	**possunt**

Chant and memorize the different forms of **possum**.

EXERCISES:

1. **Ad īnsulam natāre nōn potes.**
2. **Ad silvam ambulāre possumus.**
3. **Ad īnsulam natāre nōn potestis.**
4. **Sine pecūniā scapham aedificāre nōn possum.**
5. **Nauta puellīs fābulās saepe narrat.**
6. **Scapha nautārum prope actam est.**
7. **Puellae in casā labōrant.**
8. **Schola puellārum est prope silvam.**
9. **Scaphās spectāre amō.**
10. **Nautae īnsulās servant.**

Answers on page 181.

LATIN EXPRESSIONS

What do B.C. and A.D. mean?

The abbreviation B.C. is not Latin. It is an abbreviation of the expression *before Christ*. A.D. stands for the Latin expression **Anno Domini**. **Anno** is the ablative singular of the word **annus** which means *year*. This is a special use of the ablative case called the *ablative of time when*. Remember: The ablative case has many uses. So, **anno** means *in the year*. **Domini** is the genitive singular form of the word **dominus** which means *lord* or *master*. So, in this case, **Domini** means *of the Lord*. So literally, **Anno Domini** means *in the year of the Lord*. **Dominus**, as you have probably guessed, refers to Jesus Christ, as our years are reckoned from the traditional date of His birth.

This system of dating was invented in Rome in the sixth century A.D. by a monk named Dionysius Exiguus. Before that time there were many systems of dating. One system used the names of the two Roman consuls for that year to show what year it was. Another counted years from the founding of the city of Rome (753 B.C. according to Roman popular thought). Another method calculated the years since the beginning of the world as reckoned from the Bible. Still other systems kept track of the years by the reigns of kings and emperors. Although Dionysius Exiguus' system of numbering the years did not immediately catch on in Western Europe, more and more Europeans began to use the system until it was finally accepted by the Roman Catholic Church in the tenth century.

In academic circles the abbreviation B.C.E. is used in place of B.C. Also, the abbreviation C.E. is used in place of A.D. The abbreviation B.C.E. stands for *before the common era* and C.E. stands for *common era*. These terms are commonly used within the academic community because they do not presuppose the truth or falsehood of any belief system.

LESSON 92

CONJUGATIONS

Not every Latin verb has the same pattern of endings as the verbs you have studied so far. In Latin, there are four main patterns of verb endings called conjugations. The first conjugation, second conjugation, third conjugation, and fourth conjugation each have certain rules we must remember when adding the appropriate endings. So far, all the action verbs you know are from the first conjugation. In this book we will study only the first and second conjugations.

The following chart will help to illustrate the differences between the first and second conjugations. **Portō**, a verb you already know, is a verb of the first conjugation. **Habeō** is from the second conjugation.

	FIRST PERSON SINGULAR	INFINITIVE
FIRST CONJUGATION	**portō**	**portāre**
SECOND CONJUGATION	**habeō**	**habēre**

Notice that in the first person singular **habeō** has an *e* before the final *o*. In each of the six forms of **habeō**, there will be an *e* before the verb ending instead of an *a*. Also, **habēre**, the infinitive form of **habeō**, ends in **-ēre** instead of **-āre.** If an infinitive ends in **-āre,** that verb is from the first conjugation. If an infinitive ends in **-ēre,** that verb is from the second conjugation.

From now on when a verb is introduced, both the first person singular and the infinitive forms will be given.

LESSON 93

NEW WORD   habeō / habēre

MEANING   *I have, I do have, I am having / to have*

Habeō is a verb of the second conjugation. Study the chart below to familiarize yourself with the different forms of **habeō**. Instead of an *a* before the verb ending, **habeō** has an *e*.

Chant or sing these verb forms to memorize them.

	SINGULAR	PLURAL
FIRST PERSON	habeō	habēmus
SECOND PERSON	habēs	habētis
THIRD PERSON	habet	habent

INFINITIVE
habēre

EXERCISES:

1. **Pecūniam habeō.**
2. **Scapham habēs.**
3. **Poēta tabulam habet.**
4. **Pecūniam nōn habēmus sed nautae pecūniam habent.**
5. **Pecūniam habētis.**

118

6. Circum īnsulam nāvigāre nōn possumus.
7. Casam prope actam aedificāre dēsīderās.
8. Poēta agricolīs nautīsque fābulam narrat.
9. Incolae īnsulārum in aquā saepe natant.
10. Ad īnsulam nāvigāre nōn potestis.

Answers on page 181.

LESSON 94

NEW WORD   **quod**

MEANING   *because*

PRONUNCIATION TIP: In both classical and ecclesiastical pronunciation, **quod** rhymes with *toad, road,* and *load.*

EXERCISES:

1. Scapham habeō quod nauta sum.
2. Terram arāmus quod agricolae sumus.
3. Lūnam stellāsque spectō quod nauta sum.
4. Poēta puellīs fābulam narrat quod puellae fābulās amant.
5. In scaphā familia est quod ad patriam nāvigāre dēsīderant.
6. Sine pecūniā ad patriam nāvigāre nōn potestis.
7. Casae agricolārum sunt prope silvam.
8. Pecūnia nautae est in scaphā.
9. Fēmina cum puellīs in tabernam ambulat.
10. Poētae pecūniam dāmus.

Answers on page 181.

LESSON 95

NEW WORD   **bestia**

MEANING   *beast*

EXERCISES:

1. **Sunt bestiae in silvā.**
2. **Bestiae casās aedificāre nōn possunt.**
3. **Sine bestiīs terram arāre nōn possumus.**
4. **Bestiae silvae casās nōn habent.**
5. **Poēta nōn es.**
6. **Puella agricolīs aquam dat.**
7. **Terram arāre amō quod agricola sum.**
8. **Scapha nautae in īnsulā est.**
9. **Terram arāre nōn possumus quod bestiās nōn habēmus.**
10. **Tabulās portās.**

Answers on page 181.

LESSON 96

NEW WORD   **timeō / timēre**

MEANING   *I fear, I do fear, I am fearing / to fear*

Use this handy chart to review the endings of **timeō**.

	SINGULAR	PLURAL
FIRST PERSON	**timeō**	**timēmus**
SECOND PERSON	**timēs**	**timētis**
THIRD PERSON	**timet**	**timent**

INFINITIVE
timēre

EXERCISES:

1. **Bestiās nōn timeō.**
2. **Incolae īnsulae bestiās timent.**
3. **Puella in silvā ambulat quod bestiās nōn timet.**
4. **In silvā cum bestiīs ambulāre dēsīderō.**
5. **Bestiae agricolās nōn timent.**
6. **Bestiae nautās nōn timent sed nautae bestiās timent.**
7. **Poētae pecūniam dāmus quod pecūniam nōn habet.**
8. **Ad īnsulam nāvigāre nōn potes quod scapham nōn habēs.**
9. **In casā agricolae sum.**
10. **Aquam nōn amō quod natāre nōn possum.**

Answers on page 182.

LESSON 97

NEW WORD   **rēgīna**

MEANING   *queen*

PRONUNCIATION TIP: In classical pronunciation, the *g* in **rēgīna** sounds like the *g* in *go*. In ecclesiastical pronunciation, it will sound like the *g* in *gentle*.

EXERCISES:

1. **Rēgīnam amāmus.**
2. **Incolae silvārum rēgīnam nōn timent.**
3. **Poēta rēgīnae fābulās narrat.**
4. **Rēgīna poētīs pecūniam semper dat.**
5. **Agricolae bestiās silvae timent.**
6. **Natāre nōn potes quod es incola silvae.**
7. **Familia agricolae ad actam ambulat quod natāre amant.**
8. **Nauta scapham habet sed pecūniam nōn habet.**
9. **Casam sine pecūniā aedificāre nōn possum.**
10. **Puellae tabulās portant quod ad scholam ambulant.**

Answers on page 182.

LESSON 98

NEW WORD   **videō / vidēre**

MEANING   *I see, I do see, I am seeing / to see*

Videō is another verb of the second conjugation. Study the chart below to familiarize yourself with the different forms of **videō**.

	SINGULAR	PLURAL
FIRST PERSON	**videō**	**vidēmus**
SECOND PERSON	**vidēs**	**vidētis**
THIRD PERSON	**videt**	**vident**

INFINITIVE
vidēre

EXERCISES:

1. **Īnsulam vidēmus.**
2. **Rēgīnam vidēre nōn potestis.**
3. **Bestiās cotīdiē videō quod incola silvae sum.**
4. **Incolae silvārum bestiās nōn timent.**
5. **Sine scaphīs īnsulam servāre nōn possumus.**
6. **Rēgīna nōn es.**
7. **Agricola casam in silvā habet.**
8. **Nautae incolās īnsulārum timent.**

9. **Scaphae circum īnsulam saepe nāvigant.**
10. **Bestiae pecūniam numquam portant.**

Answers on page 182.

LATIN EXPRESSIONS

Have you ever bought something under the condition of **caveat emptor**?

Emptor means *buyer*. **Caveat** is a special kind of verb that means *let him beware* or *may he beware*. So literally, **caveat emptor** means *let the buyer beware*. This expression is used to warn potential buyers that it may be risky to purchase something because the seller is not obligated to take it back if it is defective.

Sometimes the word **caveat** is used by itself. Even though this word is a Latin verb, over time it has come to be used as a noun that means *warning*. For example:

> Dad let me go to the party, but with one **caveat** : Be home before 10:30 P.M. or be grounded for a week.

Another related expression is **cave canem**. In this case, **cave** is the form of the verb used to give a command. **Cave**, then, means *beware*! **Canem** is the accusative form of the word **canis** which means *dog*. **Cave canem** literally means *beware (of) the dog*.

If you see a sign like that, don't worry about Latin grammar—just run!

124

LESSON 99

NEW WORD **maneō / manēre**

MEANING   *I stay, I do stay, I am staying / to stay*

EXERCISES:

1. Nauta in īnsulā manēre dēsīderat.
2. Bestiae in silvā manent.
3. In aquā manēre nōn potes.
4. Patriam servāre dēsīderō quod ego rēgīna sum.
5. Nautae in īnsulā manent quod scapham nōn habent.
6. Stellās videō sed lūnam vidēre nōn possum.
7. Nautae aquam nōn timent quod natāre possunt.
8. Incolae silvae bestiās cotīdiē vident.
9. In tabernam sine pecūniā numquam ambulāmus.
10. Fābulās narrāre nōn potestis quod poētae nōn estis.

Answers on page 182.

LESSON 100

DECLENSIONS

Not all Latin nouns have the same pattern of endings as the nouns you have studied. In Latin there are five main patterns of noun endings called *declensions*. The first declension, second declension, third declension, fourth declension and fifth declension all have the same five cases, but each declension has a unique pattern of endings. In this book we will study only the first and second declensions. All of the nouns you know so far are from the first declension. Let's review those endings using the chart below.

	SINGULAR	PLURAL
NOMINATIVE (SUBJECT/PREDICATE)	-a	-ae
GENITIVE (POSSESSION)	-ae	-ārum
DATIVE (INDIRECT OBJECT)	-ae	-īs
ACCUSATIVE (DIRECT OBJECT/OBJECT OF PREP.)	-am	-ās
ABLATIVE (MANY USES)	-ā	-īs

Soon you will learn about the second declension. This means that you will have to learn another set of endings, but you will also have the opportunity to learn words found only in the second declension. With these new words, you will be able to read more interesting sentences.

LESSON 101

NEW WORD   **vir**

MEANING   *man*

In the first declension, every word in the nominative singular ends in **-a**. The second declension, however, is not like that. In the second declension, not every word will have the same ending in the nominative singular.

Vir is the first word you have seen from the second declension. We will learn the endings of the second declension step by step.

SECOND DECLENSION	SINGULAR	PLURAL
NOMINATIVE (SUBJECT/PREDICATE NOM.)	vir	
GENITIVE (POSSESSION)		
DATIVE (INDIRECT OBJECT)		
ACCUSATIVE (DIRECT OBJECT/OBJECT OF PREP.)		
ABLATIVE (MANY USES)		

EXERCISES:
1. **Vir sum.**
2. **Vir est incola īnsulae.**
3. **Vir casam habet sed scapham nōn habet.**
4. **Vir bestiās timet.**
5. **Vir incolīs īnsulārum fābulās narrat.**
6. **Vir in īnsulā manēre dēsīderat.**
7. **Ad tabernam ambulātis sed pecūniam nōn habētis.**
8. **Vir es sed fēmina sum.**
9. **Īnsulam vidēre nōn possumus.**
10. **Ā patriā ad īnsulam nāvigātis.**

Answers on page 183.

LESSON 102

NEW WORD   **virī**

MEANING   *men* (nominative plural)

SECOND DECLENSION	SINGULAR	PLURAL
NOMINATIVE (SUBJECT/PREDICATE NOM.)	**vir**	**virī**
GENITIVE (POSSESSION)		
DATIVE (INDIRECT OBJECT)		
ACCUSATIVE (DIRECT OBJECT/OBJECT OF PREP.)		
ABLATIVE (MANY USES)		

EXERCISES:

1. **Virī in casā sunt.**
2. **Virī īnsulae scaphās servant.**
3. **Vir sine scaphā ad īnsulam nāvigāre nōn potest.**
4. **Vir fēminaque saepe terram arant.**
5. **Poētae estis sed fābulās narrāre nōn amātis.**
6. **Bestiae silvārum agricolās nōn timent.**
7. **Ad patriam nāvigās sed in īnsulā maneō.**
8. **Stellās vidēmus sed lūnam vidēre nōn possumus.**
9. **Rēgīna incolās īnsulārum nōn timet.**
10. **Rēgīna poētīs pecūniam semper dat.**

Answers on page 183.

LESSON 103

NEW WORD   **virum / virōs**

MEANING   *man / men* (accusative singular and plural)

In this lesson you will learn both the accusative singular and accusative plural of **vir**.

SECOND DECLENSION	SINGULAR	PLURAL
NOMINATIVE (SUBJECT/PREDICATE NOM.)	**vir**	**virī**
GENITIVE (POSSESSION)		
DATIVE (INDIRECT OBJECT)		
ACCUSATIVE (DIRECT OBJECT/OBJECT OF PREP.)	**virum**	**virōs**
ABLATIVE (MANY USES)		

EXERCISES:

1. **Bestia virum nōn timet.**
2. **Virōs in scaphā videō.**
3. **Vir bestiās timet sed bestiae virum nōn timent.**
4. **Virī casās aedificant.**
5. **Virī pecūniam numquam habent.**
6. **Casam aedificāre nōn possum sed scaphās saepe aedificō.**
7. **Cum puellīs ad actam ambulō.**
8. **Poēta puellae fābulās narrat.**
9. **Virī īnsulārum nautīs scaphās saepe dant.**
10. **In īnsulā manēmus quod īnsulam amāmus.**

Answers on page 183.

LESSON 104

NEW WORD   **virī / virōrum**

MEANING   *man / men* (genitive singular and plural)

In this lesson you will learn both the genitive singular and genitive plural of **vir**.

SECOND DECLENSION	SINGULAR	PLURAL
NOMINATIVE (SUBJECT / PREDICATE NOM.)	vir	virī
GENITIVE (POSSESSION)	(virī)	(virōrum)
DATIVE (INDIRECT OBJECT)		
ACCUSATIVE (DIRECT OBJECT / OBJECT OF PREP.)	virum	virōs
ABLATIVE (MANY USES)		

In the first declension, the nominative plural always looks identical to the genitive singular. This is often true in the second declension, too. Also, the **-ōrum** ending of the genitive plural is very similar to the **-arum** ending of the genitive plural of the first declension.

EXERCISES:

1. **Casa virī est prope actam.**
2. **Familiae virōrum ad īnsulam nāvigant.**
3. **Scapha virī in īnsulā est.**
4. **Virī in scaphīs sunt nautae.**
5. **Vir casam in īnsulā aedificat.**
6. **Virī terram nōn arant quod labōrāre nōn amant.**
7. **Poēta tabulam dēsīderat sed pecūniam nōn habet.**
8. **Rēgīna poētae pecūniam dat.**
9. **Poēta cum rēgīnā manēre dēsīderat.**
10. **Puella ad scholam tabulās portat.**

Answers on page 183.

130

LESSON 105

NEW WORD   **virō / virīs**

MEANING   *man / men* (dative and ablative singular and plural)

In this lesson you will learn the dative and ablative forms of **vir**.

Second Declension	Singular	Plural
Nominative (subject/predicate nom.)	**vir**	**virī**
Genitive (possession)	**virī**	**virōrum**
Dative (indirect object)	**virō**	**virīs**
Accusative (direct object/object of prep.)	**virum**	**virōs**
Ablative (many uses)	**virō**	**virīs**

In the second declension, the dative plural and the ablative plural look identical. Unlike the first declension, however, the dative singular and the ablative singular of the second declension also look identical.

EXERCISES:

1. **Virō fābulam narrō.**
2. **Rēgīna virīs pecūniam dat.**
3. **In silvā cum virīs labōrāre dēsīderāmus.**
4. **Puella virīs aquam saepe dat.**
5. **Ā patriā ad īnsulam ambulāre nōn potes.**
6. **Scapha virōrum est prope actam.**
7. **Virī silvae agricolam nōn amant.**
8. **In īnsulā casam aedificās sed ego in silvā casam aedificō.**
9. **Puellae ā scholā ad tabernam cotīdiē ambulant.**
10. **Sine tabulā in scholam numquam ambulō.**

Answers on page 184.

LESSON 106

NEW WORD   **murus**

MEANING   *wall*

Murus is another noun from the second declension.

Use this handy chart to review the different forms of **murus**.

SECOND DECLENSION	SINGULAR	PLURAL
NOMINATIVE (SUBJECT / PREDICATE NOM.)	**murus**	**murī**
GENITIVE (POSSESSION)	**murī**	**murōrum**
DATIVE (INDIRECT OBJECT)	**murō**	**murīs**
ACCUSATIVE (DIRECT OBJECT / OBJECT OF PREP.)	**murum**	**murōs**
ABLATIVE (MANY USES)	**murō**	**murīs**

EXERCISES:

1. **Murum aedificō.**
2. **Circum casās murum aedificāmus.**
3. **Virī murōs aedificant.**
4. **Puella patriam amat sed ad īnsulās nāvigāre dēsīderat.**
5. **Virīs fēminīsque īnsulae pecūniam dare nōn possum quod pecūniam nōn habeō.**
6. **Cum scaphīs maneō quod virōs īnsulārum timeō.**
7. **Scaphās aedificāre amātis sed nāvigāre nōn amātis.**
8. **In casā sum quod bestiās timeō.**
9. **Scapha est in aquā sine nautīs.**
10. **Sine rēgīnā patriam servāre nōn possumus.**

Answers on page 184.

LESSON 107

NEW WORD   **deleō / delēre**

MEANING   *I destroy, I do destroy, I am destroying / to destroy*

EXERCISES:

1. **Agricolae silvam delent.**
2. **Casās scaphāsque īnsulārum delēre dēsīderō.**
3. **Scaphās nautārum delēre nōn potes quod nautae scaphās servant.**
4. **Virī patriam servāre dēsīderant.**
5. **Bestiae silvae casam delent.**
6. **Virōs fēmināsque patriae servāmus.**
7. **Rēgīna virō pecūniam dare nōn potest quod pecūniam nōn habet.**
8. **Casa virī est prope actam.**
9. **Ab īnsulā ad patriam natāre dēsīderō.**
10. **Cum puellīs ad scholam ambulāmus.**

Answers on page 184.

LESSON 108

NEW WORD **cibus**

MEANING *food*

PRONUNCIATION TIP: In classical pronunciation, the *c* in **cibus** sounds like the *k* in *kitchen*. In ecclesiastical pronunciation, it sounds like the *ch* in *cheese*.

Cibus is another noun of the second declension. It has the same endings as **murus**.

EXERCISES:

1. **Cibum portāmus.**
2. **Cibum habeō sed aquam nōn habeō.**
3. **Cibum aquamque portō.**
4. **Virī cibum aquamque portant quod ad silvam ambulant.**
5. **Fēminae poētae cibum dant quod cibum nōn habet.**
6. **Nautae cibum nōn habent.**
7. **Virī īnsulārum scaphās nautārum delent.**
8. **Murum aedificāmus quod patriam servāre dēsīderāmus.**
9. **Rēgīna virīs silvae pecūniam semper dat.**
10. **Bestiae silvae cibum dēsīderant.**

Answers on page 184.

LESSON 109

NEW WORD   **fīlius**

MEANING   *son*

Compare the nominative plural and the genitive singular of **fīlius**. It's just like the other words you know, but with one difference. The genitive singular ends with one *i* but the nominative plural has two.

SECOND DECLENSION	SINGULAR	PLURAL
NOMINATIVE (SUBJECT/PREDICATE NOM.)	**fīlius**	**fīliī**
GENITIVE (POSSESSION)	**fīlī**	**fīliōrum**
DATIVE (INDIRECT OBJECT)	**fīliō**	**fīliīs**
ACCUSATIVE (DIRECT OBJECT/OBJECT OF PREP.)	**fīlium**	**fīliōs**
ABLATIVE (MANY USES)	**fīliō**	**fīliīs**

EXERCISES:

1. **Fīlius virī in casā est.**
2. **Nautae fīliō agricolae fābulās narrant.**
3. **Fīliī agricolārum terram arant.**
4. **Fīliī nautae ad īnsulās nāvigāre dēsīderant.**
5. **Puella fīliīs agricolae aquam dat.**
6. **Sine cibō aquāque ad īnsulam nāvigāre nōn possumus.**
7. **Rēgīna in īnsulā manēre dēsīderat quod virōs patriae timet.**
8. **Natāre amō quod aquam nōn timeō.**
9. **Sine scaphā ad īnsulam nāvigāre nōn potes.**
10. **Casae virōrum sunt prope actam.**

Answers on page 185.

LESSON 110

NEW WORD   **puer**

MEANING   *boy*

Puer is another noun from the second declension.

SECOND DECLENSION	SINGULAR	PLURAL
NOMINATIVE (SUBJECT/PREDICATE NOM.)	**puer**	**puerī**
GENITIVE (POSSESSION)	**puerī**	**puerōrum**
DATIVE (INDIRECT OBJECT)	**puerō**	**puerīs**
ACCUSATIVE (DIRECT OBJECT/OBJECT OF PREP.)	**puerum**	**puerōs**
ABLATIVE (MANY USES)	**puerō**	**puerīs**

EXERCISES:

1. **Puer est fīlius poētae.**
2. **Poēta puerīs tabulās dat.**
3. **Puerī aquam portant sed terram arāre nōn amant.**
4. **Puerī ad īnsulam nāvigāre dēsīderant sed scapham nōn habent.**
5. **In silvā labōrāre nōn possum quod bestiās timeō.**
6. **Sine fīliīs agricolae terram arāre nōn possumus.**
7. **Puerīs fābulās narrāmus.**
8. **Cibum aquamque dēsīderō.**
9. **Puerī ad īnsulam cum nautīs nāvigant.**
10. **Vir lūnam vidēre nōn potest quod in casā est.**

Answers on page 185.

LESSON 111

NEW WORD **ager**

MEANING *field*

SECOND DECLENSION	SINGULAR	PLURAL
NOMINATIVE (SUBJECT/PREDICATE NOM.)	**ager**	**agrī**
GENITIVE (POSSESSION)	**agrī**	**agrōrum**
DATIVE (INDIRECT OBJECT)	**agrō**	**agrīs**
ACCUSATIVE (DIRECT OBJECT/OBJECT OF PREP.)	**agrum**	**agrōs**
ABLATIVE (MANY USES)	**agrō**	**agrīs**

Ager is a bit different from the other second declension nouns you know. The *e* in the nominative singular form of **ager** is absent in the other forms. This is because in Latin, we make all noun forms (except the nominative singular) from the stem of the genitive singular form of the noun. This stem is called the *genitive stem*. We can find the genitive stem by removing the ending from the genitive singular.

For example, if we take **agrī**, the genitive singular form of the word **ager**, and remove the ending, we are left with **agr-**. This is the genitive stem from which you may make all the remaining forms of the word by simply adding the appropriate endings.

EXERCISES:

1. **Puerī agrōs arant quod agricola labōrāre nōn potest.**
2. **Fīliī agricolae ā casā ad agrum ambulant.**
3. **Puerī pecūniam dēsīderant sed agrōs arāre nōn amant.**
4. **Bestiae silvae casās agricolārum delent.**
5. **Virī bestiās timent sed bestiae virōs nōn timent.**
6. **In īnsulā manēre dēsīderō.**

7. **Murum circum casās aedificāmus quod virōs fēmināsque patriae servāre dēsīderāmus.**
8. **Sunt agricolae puerīque in agrīs.**
9. **Ad īnsulam nāvigāre nōn possum quod scapham nōn habeō.**
10. **Sine nautīs ad īnsulam nāvigāre nōn possumus.**

Answers on page 185.

LATIN EXPRESSIONS

Are you proud to be an **alumnus** of your old **alma mater**? If you have no idea what these words mean, read on.

The term **alma mater** is used to refer to the college or university from which a person graduated. **Mater** simply means *mother*. **Alma** is an adjective that means *nurturing*. So literally, **alma mater** means *nurturing mother*.

Alumnus refers to the person who has graduated from a certain college or university. Literally, **alumnus** means *nursling* or *foster child*. The word **alumnus,** because it is masculine and singular, should be used to refer to one male graduate. Using your knowledge of the first and second declensions, can you figure out what Latin word would refer to one female graduate? Two female graduates? What about two male graduates?

LESSON 112

NEW WORD   **gladius**

MEANING   *sword*

Gladius has the same endings as **fīlius**.

EXERCISES:

1. **Gladium habeō.**
2. **Virī gladiōs habent.**
3. **Virī fēminaeque gladiōs habent sed agrōs servāre nōn possunt.**
4. **Incolae īnsulārum gladiōs habent sed scaphās habēmus.**
5. **Agrōs casāsque cotīdiē servāmus.**
6. **Bestiae silvae agricolam nōn timent.**
7. **Puer est fīlius rēgīnae.**
8. **In īnsulā manēre nōn potes quod cibum nōn habēs.**
9. **Nautae cum incolīs īnsulae sunt.**
10. **Patriam cotīdiē servāmus quod rēgīnam amāmus.**

Answers on page 185.

LESSON 113

GENDER

In Latin, every noun is either masculine, feminine, or neuter (**neuter** is a Latin word that means *neither*). Nouns of the first declension are mostly feminine. Nouns of the second declension are either masculine or neuter (you will learn more about this soon). So far, all the words you know from the second declension are masculine (words such as **vir**, **murus**, **fīlius**, **puer**, **ager,** and **gladius**).

PAIN-FUL WORDS

Although most nouns of the first declension are feminine, there are a few first declension nouns that are masculine. You already know these words: **poēta**, **agricola**, **incola**, and **nauta**. These exceptions to the rule are easy to remember because the first letter of each word spells out the word *PAIN*.

LESSON 114

NEUTER NOUNS OF THE SECOND DECLENSION

So far, we have only studied the masculine nouns of the second declension. Now, let's turn our attention to the neuter nouns of the second declension. Neuter nouns of the second declension end in **-um** in the nominative singular. As you study the chart below, notice the circled endings. These endings are different from the masculine nouns of the second declension.

SECOND DECLENSION (NEUTER)	SINGULAR	PLURAL
NOMINATIVE (SUBJECT/PREDICATE NOM.)	-um	-a
GENITIVE (POSSESSION)	-ī	-ōrum
DATIVE (INDIRECT OBJECT)	-ō	-īs
ACCUSATIVE (DIRECT OBJECT/OBJECT OF PREP.)	-um	-a
ABLATIVE (MANY USES)	-ō	-īs

As you can see from the chart, the only differences are in the nominative singular, nominative plural, and accusative plural.

LESSON 115

NEW WORD   **oppidum** (second declension neuter)

MEANING   *town*

Examine the chart below to see the endings of **oppidum**.

SECOND DECLENSION (NEUTER)	SINGULAR	PLURAL
NOMINATIVE (SUBJECT/PREDICATE NOM.)	**oppidum**	**oppida**
GENITIVE (POSSESSION)	**oppidī**	**oppidōrum**
DATIVE (INDIRECT OBJECT)	**oppidō**	**oppidīs**
ACCUSATIVE (DIRECT OBJECT/OBJECT OF PREP.)	**oppidum**	**oppida**
ABLATIVE (MANY USES)	**oppidō**	**oppidīs**

Again, the nominative singular, nominative plural, and accusative plural are different than masculine words of the second declension.

EXERCISES:

1. **In oppidum ambulō.**
2. **Nautae in oppidō sunt.**
3. **Virī murum circum oppidum aedificāre dēsīderant.**
4. **Poēta puerīs puellīsque oppidī fābulās narrat.**
5. **Virī murōs oppidī servāre dēsīderant.**
6. **Virī oppidī gladiōs habent.**
7. **Puerī estis sed virī sumus.**
8. **Oppidum servāre nōn possumus quod oppidum murōs nōn habet.**
9. **Fīlius agricolae agrōs numquam arat quod labōrāre nōn amat.**
10. **Virī silvae scaphās numquam aedificant.**

Answers on page 186.

LESSON 116

NEW WORD   **aurum, aurī** (second declension neuter)

MEANING   *gold*

EXERCISES:

1. **Ego aurum dēsīderō.**
2. **Virī silvae aurum nōn habent.**
3. **Ad patriam cum pecūniā aurōque nāvigāmus.**
4. **Nautae oppida īnsulae delent quod aurum dēsīderant.**
5. **Puerī puellaeque oppidī agrōs arāre nōn amant.**
6. **Oppidum servāmus quod incolās īnsulārum timēmus.**
7. **Fīliīs poētae cibum saepe dāmus quod pecūniam nōn habent.**
8. **Poēta fīliīs rēgīnae fābulās saepe narrat.**
9. **Fīlius rēgīnae pecūniam aurumque habet sed in agrīs cum agricolīs labōrāre dēsīderat.**
10. **Circum īnsulam natāre nōn potes.**

Answers on page 186.

LESSON 117

NEW WORD   **argentum, argentī** (second declension neuter)

MEANING   *silver*

EXERCISES:

1. **Argentum aurumque amō.**
2. **Nautae aurum ad patriam portant.**
3. **Argentum ā scaphā ad casam portāmus.**
4. **Puerī in agrīs cum virīs oppidī labōrant.**
5. **Rēgīna oppidum delēre dēsīderat.**
6. **Incolae oppidōrum bestiās silvae timent.**
7. **Aurum argentumque habētis sed cibum nōn habētis.**
8. **Sine pecūniā casās aedificāre nōn possumus.**
9. **Rēgīna murum circum oppidum aedificāre dēsīderat.**
10. **Puerī natant quod labōrāre nōn amant.**

Answers on page 186.

LESSON 118

NEW WORD   **caelum, caelī** (second declension neuter)

MEANING   *sky*

EXERCISES:

1. **Caelum spectō.**
2. **Sunt stellae in caelō.**
3. **Nautae caelum semper spectant.**
4. **Stellās in caelō numquam numerāre potes.**
5. **Īnsula aurum argentumque habet.**
6. **Caelum vidēre nōn possumus quod in casā sumus.**
7. **Incolae oppidōrum bestiās timent.**
8. **In casā maneō.**
9. **Sine scaphā ad īnsulam nāvigāre nōn potes.**
10. **Scaphae cibum ad īnsulam portant.**

Answers on page 186.

LESSON 119

NEW WORD **dōnum, dōnī** (second declension neuter)

MEANING *gift*

EXERCISES:

1. **Rēgīnae dōna dāmus.**
2. **Puellae puerīque nautīs dōna dant.**
3. **Virī fēminaeque oppidī rēgīnae pecūniam semper dant.**
4. **Puellae rēgīnae dōna dare dēsīderant.**
5. **Dōnum nautae est in scaphā.**
6. **Fīliī agricolae agrōs arant quod cibum pecūniamque dēsīderant.**
7. **Nōn es rēgīna.**
8. **Lūna est in caelō.**
9. **Cum virīs oppidī manēre dēsīderō.**
10. **Scaphae prope actam sunt.**

Answers on page 187.

LATIN EXPRESSIONS

Have you ever seen the abbreviation N.B. and wondered what it means?

The abbreviation N.B. is short for **nota bene. Nota** is a verb in the form of a command. It means *take note*! **Bene** is an adverb that means *well*. Literally, **nota bene** means *note well*. Writers use this expression to call attention to a special point or an important piece of information that the reader ought to remember.

N.B. You must study your Latin every day to improve!

LESSON 120

EXPRESSING MEANS OR INSTRUMENT

In English, we have different ways of expressing the means or instrument used to accomplish a task. Consider the following examples:

> I hit the nail <u>with a hammer</u>.
> I traveled to the island <u>by boat</u>.
> We fooled the guard <u>by means of trickery</u>.

In each of the above examples we used *with, by,* or *by means of* to express the means or instrument used to accomplish a task. In the next lesson, you will learn how to express means or instrument in Latin.

LESSON 121

ABLATIVE OF MEANS

In Latin, we use the ablative case to express means or instrument. When we use the ablative case in this way, it is called the *ablative of means*. The following examples demonstrate how the ablative of means is used:

> **Vir <u>gladiō</u> casam servat** (*The man is guarding the house <u>with a sword</u>*).
> **Nautae <u>scaphā</u> ad īnsulam nāvigant** (*The sailors are sailing to the island <u>by boat</u>*).

In each example, the item being used to accomplish the task is in the ablative case. Notice that the ablative of means shows means or instrument without the use of an additional preposition such as **cum**.

In the next lesson, you will practice using the ablative case in this way.

LESSON 122

NEW WORD   **scūtum, scūtī** (second declension neuter)

MEANING   *shield*

EXERCISES:

1. **Puer scūtum habet.**
2. **Gladiō scūtōque rēgīnam servō.**
3. **Gladiōs et scūta habēmus quod murōs oppidī servāmus.**
4. **Sine gladiīs scūtīsque patriam servāre nōn possumus.**
5. **Argentum aurumque amō sed pecūniam nōn habeō.**
6. **Incolae patriae casās aedificant.**
7. **Scaphā ad īnsulam nāvigō.**
8. **Virī oppidī fīlium rēgīnae nōn amant.**
9. **Patriam vidēre dēsīderāmus.**
10. **Virī īnsulārum patriam delēre dēsīderant.**

Answers on page 187.

LESSON 123

NEW WORD   **pugnō / pugnāre**

MEANING   *I fight, I do fight, I am fighting / to fight*

PRONUNCIATION TIP: In classical pronunciation, the *g* in **pugnō** has a hard *g* sound like the *g* in *get*. In ecclesiastical pronunciation, the *g* and the *n* together will sound like the *ny* in *canyon*. So it will sound something like *POON-yo*.

EXERCISES:

1. **Virī gladiīs scūtīsque pugnant.**
2. **Pugnāre nōn amō.**
3. **Incolae īnsulae pugnāre nōn possunt quod gladiōs nōn habent.**
4. **Gladiōs scūtaque habēmus quod oppidum servāmus.**
5. **Stellās in caelō spectāre amō.**
6. **Fīlius rēgīnae gladium dēsīderat.**
7. **Ad actam ambulō quod scaphās vidēre dēsīderō.**
8. **Cibum nōn habētis quod agrōs numquam arātis.**
9. **Fīlius agricolae es sed ego fīlius rēgīnae sum.**
10. **Lūnam stellāsque semper spectō.**

Answers on page 187.

LESSON 124

NEW WORD   **lignum, lignī** (second declension neuter)

MEANING   *wood*

PRONUNCIATION TIP: In classical pronunciation, the *g* in lignum has a hard *g* sound like the *g* in *get*. In ecclesiastical pronunciation, the *g* and the *n* together will sound like the *ny* in *canyon*. So it will sound something like *LEAN-yoom*.

EXERCISES:

1. **Lignum in casam portō.**
2. **Lignō casam aedificō.**
3. **Lignum portāre nōn amō.**
4. **Ā silvā ad oppidum lignum portāmus.**
5. **Rēgīnam vidēre dēsīderō.**
6. **Virī gladiīs patriam servant.**
7. **Murum circum oppidum aedificāmus quod bestiās timēmus.**
8. **Nautae lignō scaphās aedificant.**
9. **Puellīs oppidī dōna damus.**
10. **Sine cibō aquāque agrōs arāre nōn potes.**

Answers on page 187.

LESSON 125

NEW WORD   **saxum, saxī** (second declension neuter)

MEANING   *rock*

EXERCISES:

1. **Saxa portāmus.**
2. **Saxīs lignōque murum aedificāmus.**
3. **Virī sine lignō saxīsque casam aedificāre nōn possunt.**
4. **Virī īnsulae oppida patriae delent.**
5. **Saxa ad oppidum portāmus quod murum aedificāmus.**
6. **Cibum nōn habēs quod labōrāre nōn amās.**
7. **Virī patriae gladiīs scūtīsque cotīdiē pugnant.**
8. **Virī fēminaeque rēgīnae aurum argentumque dant.**
9. **Virī gladiōs scūtaque habent quod oppida patriae servant.**
10. **Ad patriam nāvigās sed in īnsulā maneō.**

Answers on page 188.

LATIN EXPRESSIONS

Have you ever looked closely at the back of a one-dollar bill?

The Great Seal of the United States has two sides like a coin. Both sides of the seal are shown on the back of a one-dollar bill. If you look to the right, you will notice an eagle holding a banner in its mouth. On this banner is written the expression **e pluribus unum**. **Unum** means *one*. **E** is a preposition that means *out of*. There are two forms of this preposition: **e** and **ex**. **E** is usually used if the next word begins with a consonant. **Ex** is used if the next word begins with a vowel. Since **pluribus** begins with a consonant, **e** is used here. **Pluribus** means *many*. So literally, **e pluribus unum** means *one out of many* or *one from many*. In context, this expression probably means *one nation out of many peoples*, or perhaps *one country made up of many states*.

Over the pyramid on the left you will see the phrase **annuit coeptis**. **Annuit** comes from the verb **annuo** which means to *smile on* or *approve*. When **annuo** is used this way, the noun to which it refers must be in the dative case. **Coeptis** is in the dative plural and means *beginnings* or *undertakings*. So **annuit coeptis** means *He smiled on the beginnings* or perhaps *He approved of the undertakings*. Pronouns that refer to God are sometimes capitalized, especially in some religious literature and certain versions of the Bible.

Under the pyramid is yet another phrase: **novus ordo seclorum**. **Ordo** means *order, rank* or *arrangement*. **Novus** means *new* and goes along with **ordo**. **Seclorum** is the genitive plural of the word **saeculum**. **Saeculum** can mean *generation* or *age,* as well as other things. So **novus ordo seclorum** means something like *a new order of the ages*.

That's a lot of Latin for only a dollar!

LESSON 126

ADJECTIVES

An adjective is a word that describes a noun. For example:

The <u>green</u> car
The <u>hot</u> soup
The <u>old</u> farmer

In Latin, adjectives work together with nouns in a special way. Any adjective must agree with the noun it describes in three ways: case, number, and gender. For example, if a noun is in the genitive case, any adjective that goes with that noun must also be in the genitive case. If a noun is singular, any adjective that goes with it must also be singular. If a noun is feminine, any adjective that goes with it must also have a corresponding feminine ending.

All the adjectives you will learn in this book will share the endings of the first and second declensions.

LESSON 127

NEW WORD   **validus, valida, validum**

MEANING   *strong*

Validus, valida, validum is your first Latin adjective. Adjectives are listed in masculine, feminine and neuter forms (in the nominative singular) because they may take any ending of these three genders. This and all the other adjectives you will learn about in this book use the endings of the first and second declensions. As you study the three charts below, you will notice that this adjective can use any of the endings of the first declension, second declension masculine, and second declension neuter.

SECOND DECLENSION (MASCULINE)	SINGULAR	PLURAL
NOMINATIVE (SUBJECT/PREDICATE NOM.)	**validus**	**validī**
GENITIVE (POSSESSION)	**validī**	**validōrum**
DATIVE (INDIRECT OBJECT)	**validō**	**validīs**
ACCUSATIVE (DIRECT OBJECT/OBJECT OF PREP.)	**validum**	**validōs**
ABLATIVE (MANY USES)	**validō**	**validīs**

FEMININE	SINGULAR	PLURAL
NOMINATIVE (SUBJECT/PREDICATE NOM.)	**valida**	**validae**
GENITIVE (POSSESSION)	**validae**	**validārum**
DATIVE (INDIRECT OBJECT)	**validae**	**validīs**
ACCUSATIVE (DIRECT OBJECT/OBJECT OF PREP.)	**validam**	**validās**
ABLATIVE (MANY USES)	**validā**	**validīs**

Second Declension (neuter)	Singular	Plural
Nominative (subject/predicate nom.)	validum	valida
Genitive (possession)	validī	validōrum
Dative (indirect object)	validō	validīs
Accusative (direct object/object of prep.)	validum	valida
Ablative (many uses)	validō	validīs

In Latin, an adjective must be in the same case, number, and gender as the word it describes. Also, remember that an adjective usually comes after the word it describes. Here are some examples of how adjectives are used:

> **Vir validus est in agrō** (*The strong man is in the field*).
> **Fēmina est valida** (*The woman is strong*).
> **Scūtum validum virum servat** (*The strong shield is guarding the man*).
> **Puerum validum spectō** (*I am watching the strong boy*).
> **Scūta valida habēmus** (*We have strong shields*).

Now try to translate a few on your own.

EXERCISES:

1. **Fēmina est valida.**
2. **Vir est validus.**
3. **Lignum est validum.**
4. **Puerī validī agrōs arant.**
5. **Fēminae validae aquam portant.**
6. **Murum validum aedificāmus.**
7. **Cum virīs validīs patriae maneō.**
8. **Puella valida lignum saepe portat.**
9. **Virī puerīque oppidī lignum saxaque portant quod murum validum aedificāre dēsīderant.**
10. **Bestiam nōn timēs quod gladium scūtumque habēs.**

Answers on page 188.

LESSON 128

PAIN-FUL WORDS REVISITED

Although most nouns of the first declension are feminine, there are four common words of the first declension that are masculine. You already know these words: **poēta**, **agricola**, **incola**, and **nauta**. These exceptions to the rule are easy to remember because the first letter of each word spells out the word *PAIN*. Most other first declension nouns are feminine.

So why am I bringing this up again? Because it affects the way we use adjectives with these words. Since **poēta**, **agricola**, **incola**, and **nauta** are masculine, any adjective that describes them must be masculine, too. Use the masculine endings of the second declension for adjectives that go with these words. Observe the examples below:

> **Agricola validus** *(the strong farmer)*

In this example, **agricola** is in the nominative singular. But instead of the feminine **valida** to go with it, **agricola** needs the masculine **validus**.

> **Scapha nautae validī** *(the strong sailor's boat)*

In this example, **nautae** is in the genitive singular. But instead of the feminine **validae** to go with it, **nautae** needs the masculine **validī**.

Using the chart below, study the way adjectives are used with masculine nouns of the first declension.

	SINGULAR	PLURAL
NOMINATIVE	agricola validus	agricolae validī
GENITIVE	agricolae validī	agricolārum validōrum
DATIVE	agricolae validō	agricolīs validīs
ACCUSATIVE	agricolam validum	agricolās validōs
ABLATIVE	agricolā validō	agricolīs validīs

LESSON 129

NEW WORD   **laetus, laeta, laetum**

MEANING   *happy*

As you translate these exercises, keep in mind that although **poēta**, **agricola**, **incola**, and **nauta** are in the first declension, they are masculine, and any adjective that goes with these nouns must have a masculine ending.

Remember also that an adjective usually comes after the noun it describes.

EXERCISES:

1. **Puellae sunt laetae.**
2. **Nauta nōn est laetus.**
3. **Agricola bestiīs validīs agrum arat.**
4. **Poēta puerīs laetīs fābulās narrat.**
5. **Familia agricolae est laeta quod cibum pecūniamque habent.**
6. **Fīliī agricolae sunt validī sed labōrāre nōn amant.**
7. **Stellās in caelō spectāre amō.**
8. **Sine virīs validīs agrōs arāre nōn potestis.**
9. **Puellae sunt laetae quod ad actam ambulant.**
10. **Rēgīna nōn est laeta quod bestiae patriam delent.**

Answers on page 188.

LESSON 130

NEW WORD   **malus, mala, malum**

MEANING   *bad*

EXERCISES:

1. **Fīlius agricolae est puer malus.**
2. **Rēgīna mala casās agricolārum delēre dēsīderat.**
3. **Puerī malī in agrīs numquam labōrant.**
4. **Poēta fābulās malās nōn amat.**
5. **Virī malī oppidum delēre nōn possunt quod oppidum servāmus.**
6. **Fēminae validae saxa ab agrīs ad actam portant.**
7. **Rēgīnam vidēre dēsīderāmus quod cibum nōn habēmus.**
8. **Puerī malī saepe pugnant.**
9. **Sine cibō aquāque in īnsulā manēre nōn potestis.**
10. **Virī fēminaeque rēgīnae dōna dant.**

Answers on page 188.

LESSON 131

NEW WORD   **fīlia, fīliae** (feminine, irregular)

MEANING   *daughter*

Study this chart for the word **fīlia**:

FIRST DECLENSION (IRREGULAR)	SINGULAR	PLURAL
NOMINATIVE (SUBJECT/PREDICATE)	**fīlia**	**fīliae**
GENITIVE (POSSESSION)	**fīliae**	**fīliārum**
DATIVE (INDIRECT OBJECT)	**fīliae**	**fīliābus**
ACCUSATIVE (DIRECT OBJECT/OBJECT OF PREP.)	**fīliam**	**fīliās**
ABLATIVE (MANY USES)	**fīliā**	**fīliābus**

Fīlia is what we call an irregular word. Irregular words have endings that do not fit the expected pattern. If you continue to study Latin, you will run into many irregular nouns and verbs.

Fīlia is irregular for a very good reason. If the dative plural and ablative plural had the normal ending **-īs**, you would not be able to tell them apart from the dative plural and ablative plural of **fīlius**, the second declension word that means *son*.

EXERCISES:

1. **Fīlia mala rēgīnae patriam delēre dēsīderat.**
2. **Fīliae agricolae sunt validae quod aquam cotīdiē portant.**
3. **Virī oppidī lignō saxīsque casam aedificant.**
4. **Puerī patriae pugnāre nōn amant sed patriam servāre dēsīderant.**
5. **Agricola nōn est laetus quod agrum arāre nōn potest.**
6. **Lignō casam aedificāmus.**

7. Poēta fīliābus agricolae fābulās narrat.
8. Fīliōs fīliāsque rēgīnae servō.
9. Rēgīna mala virīs fēminīsque patriae dōna numquam dat.
10. Sumus validī quod gladiōs scūtaque habēmus.

Answers on page 189.

LESSON 132

NEW WORD   **māgnus, māgna, māgnum**

MEANING   *great, large*

PRONUNCIATION TIP: In classical pronunciation, the *g* in **magnus** has a hard *g* sound like the *g* in *get*. In ecclesiastical pronunciation, the *g* and the *n* together will sound like the *ny* in *canyon*. So it will sound something like *MONN-yoose*.

In Latin, an adjective usually comes after the word it describes. However, an adjective of quantity or size (such as **māgnus**) usually goes before the noun it describes.

You must decide on your own whether to translate **māgnus** as *great* or *large*.

EXERCISES:

1. **Fīlius rēgīnae est māgnus vir.**
2. **Māgnī virī patriae oppidum servant.**
3. **In māgnā īnsulā manēre nōn potes quod cibum nōn habēs.**
4. **Patria māgnam rēgīnam habet.**
5. **Nauta māgnam familiam habet.**
6. **Casa agricolae nōn est māgna.**
7. **Caelum spectāmus quod stellās vidēre amāmus.**
8. **Puerī validī in agrīs labōrant sed nōn sunt laetī.**
9. **Māgnae bestiae silvārum casās agricolārum delent.**
10. **Nautae incolīs īnsulae pecūniam semper dant.**

Answers on page 189.

LESSON 133

NEW WORD   **superō / superāre**

MEANING   *I conquer, I do conquer, I am conquering / to conquer*

EXERCISES:

1. **Māgnās īnsulās superāre dēsīderō quod argentum aurumque habent.**
2. **Fīliī malī rēgīnae silvam superant.**
3. **Gladiīs scūtīsque incolās īnsulārum superāmus.**
4. **Virī īnsulārum patriam superant.**
5. **Murus validus oppidum servat.**
6. **Virī fēminaeque patriae nōn sunt laetī quod cibum numquam habent.**
7. **Sine cibō aquāque māgnōs virōs silvae pugnāre nōn potes.**
8. **Rēgīnae īnsulārum dōna semper dāmus.**
9. **Fīliī rēgīnae oppida servant quod patriam amant.**
10. **In agrīs labōrāre nōn amō sed agrōs cotīdiē arō.**

Answers on page 189.

LATIN EXPRESSIONS

Have you ever written **P.S.** at the end of a letter so you could add a final note?

The abbreviation **P.S.** is short for **post scriptum**. **Post** is a preposition that means *after*. **Scriptum** means *that which has been written*. Literally, **post scriptum** means *after that which has been written.*

P.S. Don't forget to do your Latin homework.

LESSON 134

NEW WORD   **multus, multa, multum**

MEANING   *much, many*

Multus, multa, multum can mean:

- *much* (as in quantity, when used with a singular word)
- *many* (as in number, when used with a plural word)

Remember that an adjective of quantity or size (such as **multus, multa, multum**) usually goes before the noun it describes. And, as usual, use the translation that makes the most sense in context.

EXERCISES:

1. **Multum argentum habēmus.**
2. **Sine multīs scaphīs īnsulās superāre nōn possumus.**
3. **Patria multa oppida habet.**
4. **Māgnīs saxīs murum validum aedificāre dēsīderō.**
5. **Sine multīs agricolīs agrōs arāre nōn possumus.**
6. **Nauta fīliam rēgīnae amat.**
7. **Fīliae rēgīnae sunt laetae quod multum aurum habent.**
8. **Sunt multae fēminae in īnsulā.**
9. **Fīliābus rēgīnae multa dōna dāmus.**
10. **Rēgīna multōs fīliōs habet.**

Answers on page 189.

GENERAL ADVICE

Congratulations! You have made it all the way to the end of this book. In closing, I would like to offer a few thoughts which you, the reader, may find helpful. These tips and observations should prove useful as you continue your study of Latin.

First, a translation tip: When translating Latin, your mind must be awake and alert. Why? Because one word can mean several different things. As you already know from experience, the word **nautae** can be nominative plural, genitive singular, or dative singular. So when you read Latin, think of all the case possibilities for each noun and let your mind quickly analyze each possibility in light of the context of the sentence. Latin sentences can often be like jigsaw puzzles that you must put together. Your mind should analyze and process each word, trying to arrive at the correct way to fit that word in with the other words of the sentence. This can be difficult at first, but you will improve gradually with practice.

It is often mentioned that the study of Latin improves one's knowledge of English vocabulary. Another great advantage to the study of Latin is that it sharpens the mind by building logical thinking skills. In addition, learning Latin also builds awareness of grammatical and linguistic concepts. The knowledge you gain from your efforts will benefit you as you approach other subjects such as English, history, philosophy, and religion.

Another tip: Someone who is accustomed to running a distance of only one or two miles probably will not suddenly try to run a marathon. It is the same with Latin. Don't frustrate yourself by trying to read Latin that is much too difficult for you. In more advanced Latin, the sentences may be quite long and complicated. Also, there may be words and grammatical structures that you have not studied yet. Of course, it is good to give yourself a challenge, but not something so difficult that you end up feeling discouraged. Therefore, try to read Latin texts that are on your reading level.

Please take a moment to reflect on all you have learned. Although you have come a long way from lesson 1, there is still much to learn. I hope this book has been enjoyable and profitable for you, and that the things you have learned from this book will become the foundation of a lifetime of enjoyment of the Latin language.

ANSWER KEY

LESSON THREE

1. *I am.*
2. *I am a sailor.*

LESSON FOUR

1. *I am a sailor.*
2. *I am a sailor.*

LESSON FIVE

1. *I am.*
2. *I am.*
3. *I am a sailor.*
4. *I am a sailor.*
5. *I am a sailor.*
6. *I am a sailor.*
7. *I am a sailor.*

LESSON SIX

1. *I am a farmer.*
2. *I am a farmer.*
3. *I am a farmer.*
4. *I am a farmer.*
5. *I am a sailor.*
6. *I am a sailor.*
7. *I am a sailor.*
8. *I am a sailor.*

LESSON SEVEN

1. I
2. you
3. she
4. Fred
5. Chicago
6. children
7. car
8. oatmeal
9. Switzerland
10. Grandfather

LESSON EIGHT

1. *The sailor and the farmer*
2. *The farmer and the sailor*
3. *I am a sailor.*
4. *I am a sailor.*
5. *I am both a farmer and a sailor.*
6. *I am both a sailor and a farmer.*

LESSON NINE

1. she (subject) walks (verb)
2. car (subject) is (verb)
3. I (subject) see (verb)
4. he (subject) bought (verb)
5. Sam (subject) loves (verb)
6. they (subject) swim (verb)
7. books (subject) are (verb)
8. I (subject) called (verb)
9. China (subject) produces (verb)
10. dog (subject) barks (verb)

LESSON TEN

1. *I am not.*
2. *I am not.*
3. *I am not a sailor.*
4. *I am not a sailor.*
5. *I am not a farmer.*
6. *I am not a farmer.*
7. *I am both a sailor and a farmer.*
8. *I am both a farmer and a sailor.*

LESSON ELEVEN

1. *You are.*
2. *You are not.*
3. *You are a farmer.*
4. *You are a farmer.*
5. *You are not a farmer.*
6. *You are not a farmer.*
7. *I am a farmer.*
8. *I am not a sailor.*
9. *You are both a sailor and a farmer.*
10. *I am a sailor and you are a farmer.*

LESSON TWELVE

1. *You are a poet.*
2. *You are a poet.*
3. *You are not a poet.*
4. *You are not a poet.*
5. *I am both a farmer and a poet.*
6. *I am both a sailor and a farmer.*
7. *I am a sailor.*
8. *You are not a sailor.*
9. *I am not a poet.*
10. *I am a farmer and you are a poet.*

LESSON 13

1. *He is a poet.*
2. *He is a poet.*
3. *He is a sailor.*
4. *He is a sailor.*
5. *He is not a farmer.*
6. *You are not a sailor.*
7. *You are not a farmer.*
8. *I am not.*
9. *I am both a farmer and a poet.*
10. *I am not a sailor.*

LESSON 14

1. *The farmer is a poet.*
2. *The sailor is a poet.*
3. *He is a sailor.*
4. *The poet is not a sailor.*
5. *He is not a sailor.*
6. *The poet is a farmer.*
7. *The sailor is not a farmer.*
8. *You are not a poet.*
9. *I am not a farmer.*
10. *You are both a farmer and a poet.*

LESSON 15

1. car (singular)
2. we (plural)
3. flowers (plural)
4. I (singular)
5. they (plural)
6. Jimmy (singular)
7. team (singular)
8. Mary (singular)
9. they (plural)
10. houses (plural)

LESSON 16

1. **agricolae**
2. **poētae**

LESSON 17

1. *We are.*
2. *We are sailors.*
3. *We are sailors.*
4. *We are not farmers.*
5. *We are not farmers.*
6. *We are farmers and poets.*
7. *You are not a poet.*
8. *I am a poet.*
9. *The poet is a sailor.*
10. *He is a sailor.*

LESSON 18

1. *Y'all are.*
2. *Y'all are farmers.*
3. *Y'all are farmers.*
4. *Y'all are not poets.*
5. *We are poets and y'all are sailors.*
6. *Y'all are both sailors and poets.*
7. *You are not a poet.*
8. *The farmer is a poet.*
9. *I am a poet.*
10. *He is a sailor.*

LESSON 19

1. *They are poets.*
2. *The poets are farmers.*
3. *They are not farmers.*
4. *The poets are sailors.*
5. *He is a poet.*
6. *Y'all are poets.*
7. *The sailors are not farmers.*
8. *The farmer is a poet.*
9. *We are sailors.*
10. *You are not a poet.*

LESSON 21

1. I (first person singular)
2. you (second person singular)
3. she (third person singular)
4. we (first person plural)
5. y'all (second person plural)
6. they (third person plural)
7. he (third person singular)
8. it (third person singular)
9. y'all (second person plural)
10. flowers (third person plural)

LESSON 22

1. newspaper
2. movie
3. trombone
4. baseball
5. fish
6. radio
7. building
8. speech
9. wallet
10. deer

LESSON 23

1. **nautam** (direct object)
2. **nauta** (predicate nominative)
3. **nauta** (subject)
4. **nautam** (direct object)
5. **nauta** (subject)
6. **nauta** (subject)
7. **nautam** (direct object)
8. **nauta** (predicate nominative)
9. **nautam** (direct object)
10. **nauta** (predicate nominative)

LESSON 24

1. *I am watching the sailor.*
2. *I am watching the sailor.*
3. *I am not watching the farmer.*
4. *I am watching the farmer.*
5. *I am watching the poet.*
6. *I am watching the poet.*
7. *I am watching both the sailor and the farmer.*
8. *I am not a sailor.*
9. *They are farmers.*
10. *Y'all are not poets.*

LESSON 25

1. *I am watching the sailors.*
2. *I am watching the sailors.*
3. *I am not watching the farmers.*
4. *I am watching the farmers.*
5. *I am watching the poets.*
6. *I am watching the sailor and the farmers.*
7. *I am watching the farmer.*
8. *You are a poet.*
9. *He is a sailor.*
10. *The poets are farmers.*

LESSON 26

1. *I am watching the star.*
2. *I am not watching the stars.*
3. *I am watching the star.*
4. *I am watching the stars.*
5. *They are sailors.*
6. *Y'all are not farmers.*
7. *We are poets.*
8. *I am watching both the farmers and the sailors.*
9. *The sailor is not a poet.*
10. *You are a farmer.*

LESSON 27

1. *I am watching the moon.*
2. *I am watching the stars.*
3. *I am watching both the moon and the stars.*
4. *I am watching both the stars and the moon.*
5. *The moon is not a star.*
6. *He is a poet and I am a farmer.*
7. *I am watching the sailors.*
8. *Y'all are not farmers.*
9. *We are poets.*
10. *The farmers are poets.*

LESSON 28

1. *You are watching the moon.*
2. *You are watching the stars.*
3. *You are watching both the moon and the stars.*
4. *You are watching both the sailors and the farmers.*
5. *I am watching both the sailors and the farmers.*
6. *I am not watching the stars.*
7. *We are not poets.*
8. *You are a farmer.*
9. *They are not farmers.*
10. *The sailor is not a poet.*

LESSON 29

1. *He is watching the moon.*
2. *The sailor is watching the stars.*
3. *He is watching the stars and the moon.*
4. *The farmer is not watching the stars.*
5. *The farmer is watching the sailor.*
6. *You are watching the moon.*
7. *I am watching both the poet and the farmer.*
8. *Y'all are not farmers.*
9. *He is a farmer.*
10. *The sailors are poets.*

LESSON 30

1. *We are watching the farmers.*
2. *We are not watching the poet.*
3. *He is watching the stars.*
4. *You are watching both the moon and the stars.*
5. *They are not sailors.*
6. *I am not watching the moon.*
7. *You are a farmer and I am a sailor.*
8. *The poet is a farmer.*
9. *You are not a sailor.*
10. *We are poets.*

LESSON 31

1. *Y'all are watching the star.*
2. *Y'all are watching the farmers.*
3. *Y'all are watching the sailors.*
4. *We are watching the moon.*
5. *The farmer is watching the poet.*
6. *You are watching both the moon and the stars.*
7. *He is not watching the sailors.*
8. *We are farmers.*
9. *Y'all are not sailors.*
10. *He is a farmer.*

LESSON 32

1. *They are watching the poets.*
2. *The poets are watching the stars.*
3. *The sailors are watching both the moon and the stars.*
4. *You are watching the farmer.*
5. *I am watching the moon.*
6. *Y'all are watching the sailor.*
7. *They are farmers.*
8. *I am not a sailor.*
9. *You are a farmer.*
10. *The farmer is a poet.*

LESSON 34

1. *I often watch the stars.*
2. *They often watch the stars.*
3. *You often watch the poet.*
4. *He is a poet.*
5. *Y'all are farmers.*
6. *The poet is not a farmer.*
7. *We often watch both the moon and the stars.*
8. *The farmers are poets.*
9. *We are poets.*
10. *Y'all do not often watch the moon.*

LESSON 35

1. *I am counting the stars.*
2. *You are counting the stars.*
3. *The sailor is counting the stars.*
4. *We often count the stars.*
5. *Y'all are counting the sailors.*
6. *The sailors often count the stars.*
7. *The farmers are not poets.*
8. *They are sailors.*
9. *We are farmers.*
10. *You are a poet.*

LESSON 36

1. *I am counting the money.*
2. *We often count the money.*
3. *They are watching the moon.*
4. *Y'all are counting the money.*
5. *I am a farmer.*
6. *The sailors often count the stars.*
7. *The farmer is counting the money.*
8. *Y'all are poets.*
9. *The sailor is not a farmer.*
10. *You often count the money.*

LESSON 37

1. *I am carrying money.*
2. *We are carrying money.*
3. *Both the sailors and farmers are carrying money.*
4. *He often carries money.*
5. *Y'all are not poets.*
6. *Y'all are carrying money.*
7. *You often carry money.*
8. *You are counting the stars.*
9. *They are farmers.*
10. *He is a sailor.*

LESSON 38

1. *She is a woman.*
2. *We are women.*
3. *I am a woman.*
4. *The woman is carrying money.*
5. *They are not carrying money.*
6. *He is a farmer.*
7. *I do not often count the money.*
8. *You are a farmer.*
9. *The sailors are poets.*
10. *We are watching the moon.*

LESSON 39

1. *I always carry money.*
2. *You always carry money.*
3. *The sailors always watch both the moon and the stars.*
4. *The woman often counts the money.*
5. *You are not a farmer.*
6. *They are women.*
7. *Y'all always carry money.*
8. *She is a woman.*
9. *Y'all are sailors.*
10. *We often watch the stars.*

LESSON 40

1. *I am carrying a writing tablet.*
2. *You are carrying writing tablets.*
3. *The poets always carry writing tablets.*
4. *The women often carry money.*
5. *The moon is not a star.*
6. *We are counting the money.*
7. *Y'all are watching both the stars and the moon.*
8. *Y'all are women.*
9. *The woman is watching the money.*
10. *You are a woman.*

LESSON 41

1. *I am carrying water.*
2. *The women are carrying water.*
3. *The poet often carries a writing tablet.*
4. *They are not carrying water.*
5. *Y'all are counting the money.*
6. *The sailors often watch the water.*
7. *We always count the money.*
8. *We are not poets.*
9. *They are sailors.*
10. *You are not a farmer.*

LESSON 42

1. *Y'all are girls.*
2. *The girls are counting the money.*
3. *We are counting the girls.*
4. *They are not poets.*
5. *The girls often count the stars.*
6. *The poet always carries writing tablets.*
7. *I am a woman.*
8. *Y'all are watching the farmers.*
9. *The girl is carrying water.*
10. *You are watching the moon.*

LESSON 43

1. *The women do not like the farmer.*
2. *The girl loves the sailor.*
3. *We love the poet.*
4. *I love both the moon and the stars.*
5. *The girl often carries water.*
6. *I am a girl.*
7. *Y'all always carry money.*
8. *We are women and they are girls.*
9. *I am not a sailor.*
10. *We are counting the stars.*

LESSON 44

1. *I love the forest.*
2. *The girls love the forest.*
3. *The sailor does not like the forest.*
4. *Y'all love the forest.*
5. *We are sailors and y'all are farmers.*
6. *We always carry writing tablets.*
7. *I often carry water.*
8. *The girl is watching the sailors.*
9. *We are watching the moon.*
10. *The farmer is a poet.*

LESSON 45

1. *The sailor loves boats.*
2. *You love boats.*
3. *The girl is watching both the boats and the sailors.*
4. *The sailors often count the boats.*
5. *Y'all are counting the stars.*
6. *You are a woman.*
7. *The boat is carrying the sailors.*
8. *They are girls.*
9. *Y'all love the forest.*
10. *We are not carrying water.*

LESSON 46

1. *I never carry water.*
2. *The woman never carries writing tablets.*
3. *The sailors always watch the boats.*
4. *I always count the money.*
5. *You never watch the moon.*
6. *Y'all often watch the stars.*
7. *The girl loves the forest.*
8. *Y'all are poets.*
9. *We are sailors and we love boats.*
10. *I am not a sailor.*

LESSON 47

1. *I am a farmer and I love the soil.*
2. *The farmers love the soil.*
3. *The sailor does not like the farmer.*
4. *The sailor loves boats.*
5. *They love the forest.*
6. *Y'all are watching both the moon and the stars.*
7. *He is not a farmer.*
8. *You never carry a writing tablet.*
9. *You often count the money.*
10. *You are a girl.*

LESSON 48

1. *I am a farmer but I love boats.*
2. *The woman is carrying money but the girls are carrying water.*
3. *I am a sailor but I do not like boats.*
4. *The farmer is a poet.*
5. *The farmer does not like the forest.*
6. *They are watching the boats.*
7. *The girls never carry water.*
8. *The sailor loves the forest.*
9. *We are counting the stars.*
10. *You are not a farmer.*

LESSON 49

1. *I am plowing the soil.*
2. *The farmers are plowing the soil.*
3. *The girl often plows the soil.*
4. *You never plow the soil.*
5. *The sailors love boats.*
6. *We are farmers but we love boats.*
7. *You are not a poet but you often carry writing tablets.*
8. *Y'all are farmers but y'all never plow the soil.*
9. *They are sailors but we are poets.*
10. *The poets always carry writing tablets.*

LESSON 50

1. *We are walking.*
2. *The woman is walking.*
3. *The sailors are carrying money.*
4. *Y'all do not often plow the soil.*
5. *The sailors often count the money.*
6. *I am watching the moon but you are watching the stars.*
7. *You are a sailor but I am a poet.*
8. *We are not carrying writing tablets.*
9. *The women love the forest.*
10. *They are sailors but they do not like boats.*

LESSON 51

1. *I am walking to the forest.*
2. *The sailors are walking to the boats.*
3. *You are walking to the forest but I am walking to the water.*
4. *We are carrying the money to the boat.*
5. *They are carrying the boat to the water.*
6. *The farmer always plows the soil.*
7. *You never walk to the forest.*
8. *I love the soil but I am not a farmer.*
9. *They are poets but they never carry writing tablets.*
10. *I am not a woman.*

LESSON 52

1. *I am walking to the seashore.*
2. *The sailor is walking to the seashore.*
3. *I love the seashore.*
4. *We are walking to the seashore.*
5. *The girls often walk to the forest.*
6. *You are a sailor but you do not like boats.*
7. *Y'all are not farmers but y'all often plow the soil.*
8. *You often carry a writing tablet.*
9. *The girl is walking to the seashore.*
10. *He is not a poet.*

LESSON 53

1. *We are walking to the house.*
2. *The farmer is carrying water to the houses.*
3. *They are walking to the house.*
4. *We love both the seashore and the forest.*
5. *We are poets but we do not carry writing tablets.*
6. *The farmers are plowing the soil.*
7. *They are poets.*
8. *You are not a sailor.*
9. *The sailors are poets.*
10. *They are walking to the seashore.*

LESSON 55

1. *I sail often.*
2. *The poet never sails.*
3. *The sailors are sailing.*
4. *Y'all are walking to the house.*
5. *We are not walking to the seashore.*
6. *Y'all are sailing but we are walking.*
7. *Y'all are sailors but we are poets.*
8. *The girl loves the forest.*
9. *I do not like boats and I do not like the water.*
10. *You are a sailor but you never sail.*

LESSON 56

1. *I am sailing to the island.*
2. *They often sail to the island.*
3. *The sailors often sail to the islands.*
4. *The woman loves the islands but she does not like boats.*
5. *You do not often sail to the island.*
6. *The boats are sailing to the island.*
7. *Y'all are carrying the boat to the seashore.*
8. *I am a sailor but I never sail.*
9. *The farmer does not like the house.*
10. *They are counting the money.*

LESSON 57

1. *I am sailing around the island.*
2. *We often walk around the forest.*
3. *The sailors always sail around the island.*
4. *We are walking to the house.*
5. *I am not a farmer but I often plow the soil.*
6. *You are not a poet but you always carry writing tablets.*
7. *You often watch both the stars and the moon.*
8. *The sailor loves boats.*
9. *We are not farmers but we love the soil.*
10. *I love both the seashore and the forest.*

LESSON 58

1. *I am swimming to the island.*
2. *The sailors are swimming to the island.*
3. *You are swimming but I am walking.*
4. *I love the water but I never swim.*
5. *The woman often swims around the island.*
6. *The sailor is swimming to the boat.*
7. *Y'all are farmers.*
8. *We are sailing around the islands.*
9. *Y'all always walk to the forest.*
10. *The girl loves boats but she is not a sailor.*

LESSON 59

1. *They are walking near the seashore.*
2. *The house is not near the forest.*
3. *We are sailing near the islands.*
4. *The boats never sail around the islands.*
5. *You are near the forest.*
6. *I always watch the boats.*
7. *The women and the girls are near the forest.*
8. *Y'all are carrying water.*
9. *We always swim near the island.*
10. *He is not a sailor but he loves boats.*

LESSON 60

1. *I love the homeland.*
2. *We are sailing to the homeland.*
3. *The sailor loves the homeland.*
4. *The boat is carrying the sailors to the homeland.*
5. *The woman is swimming around the island.*
6. *The homeland is an island.*
7. *You love the seashore but I love the forest.*
8. *The sailors are watching the stars and the moon.*
9. *Y'all are not farmers.*
10. *The house is near the water.*

LESSON 61

1. *I often long for the homeland.*
2. *The farmers are longing for water.*
3. *The women are longing for the seashore.*
4. *The girl is swimming to the seashore.*
5. *The boats are sailing around the island.*
6. *The farmer loves the soil.*
7. *You are not a poet.*
8. *Y'all always want money.*
9. *The farmer never carries a writing tablet.*
10. *We are near the island.*

LESSON 63

1. *I am in the house.*
2. *The sailor is on the island.*
3. *The sailors are not in the boat.*
4. *We are on the island.*
5. *The farmer is walking around the house.*
6. *We often sail to the island.*
7. *The woman is in the house but the farmer is walking into the forest.*
8. *We are longing for the homeland.*
9. *The girl is swimming near the island.*
10. *You are not a poet but you carry writing tablets.*

LESSON 64

1. *The farmers are in the houses.*
2. *The sailors are not in the boats.*
3. *The sailor is carrying the boat into the water.*
4. *The boats are in the water.*
5. *The sailor is on the island.*
6. *The sailor is sailing to the homeland.*
7. *I am not a sailor but I love boats.*
8. *The girls always walk to the seashore.*
9. *Y'all often swim near the island.*
10. *The sailor wants a boat.*

LESSON 65

1. *The school is in the forest.*
2. *The girls are walking to the school.*
3. *The girl is in the school.*
4. *The girl is carrying a writing tablet to the school.*
5. *You are a sailor but you do not like boats.*
6. *I am a sailor but you are a farmer.*
7. *We are sailing to the islands but we are longing for the homeland.*
8. *We are farmers but we never plow the soil.*
9. *The boat is in the water.*
10. *Y'all are in the boats but I am in the water.*

LESSON 66

1. *There are girls in the house.*
2. *There is a boat near the seashore.*
3. *I never swim near the island.*
4. *Y'all are longing for the forest but we like boats.*
5. *You do not like the islands.*
6. *There are both farmers and women in the houses.*
7. *The poet loves the land and the water.*
8. *The women often walk in the forests.*
9. *There is money in the boat.*
10. *I am not a farmer but I love the soil.*

LESSON 67

1. *We walk to the seashore daily.*
2. *The sailors sail around the island daily.*
3. *The farmer plows the soil daily.*
4. *The girls walk to the school daily.*
5. *We carry water to the houses daily.*
6. *There are sailors on the islands.*
7. *Y'all are poets but we are farmers.*
8. *Y'all are watching the moon but we are watching the stars.*
9. *You are longing for the homeland but I am longing for the islands.*
10. *The poet is walking into the house.*

LESSON 68

1. *The girl is walking from the house to the school.*
2. *The boats sail from the island to the homeland daily.*
3. *The woman counts the money daily.*
4. *There are farmers in the house.*
5. *We are sailing from the island to the homeland.*
6. *The sailors are not on the island.*
7. *We walk to the seashore daily.*
8. *I am sailing around the island.*
9. *Y'all are farmers but y'all never plow the soil.*
10. *The woman is carrying writing tablets.*

LESSON 69

1. The woman is in the house with the girls.
2. The farmer is not with the sailors.
3. I am walking to the seashore with the sailors.
4. The women are in the boat with the sailors.
5. The girls walk from the school to the seashore daily.
6. He is a farmer.
7. The sailors are in the boats and on the island.
8. I love the soil but I am not a farmer.
9. The girls are walking into the school with writing tablets.
10. I am in the boat but you are in the water.

LESSON 70

1. We are walking into the shop.
2. The girls walk from the school to the shop daily.
3. The money is in the boat with the sailors.
4. I am longing for the homeland.
5. There are sailors in the boats.
6. The boat often sails around the island.
7. Y'all are sailors but y'all do not like the water.
8. You never swim in the water.
9. The poet always carries writing tablets.
10. We are not near the forest.

LESSON 71

1. The woman never walks to the shop without money.
2. The sailors are on the island without a boat.
3. You are a sailor.
4. The girls are on the island but I am in the boat.
5. The sailor is on the island but he is longing for the homeland.
6. The poet walks to the seashore daily.
7. The farmer loves the homeland.
8. We are walking from the school to the seashore.
9. Y'all never plow the soil but I plow the soil daily.
10. The woman is walking into the forest with the girls.

LESSON 73

1. The sailor's money
2. The farmer's house
3. We are in the sailor's boat.
4. You are carrying the farmer's money.
5. The girl walks to the farmer's house daily.
6. We are carrying the boat from the house to the seashore.
7. We love the islands but y'all love the forest.
8. The poet is in the house with the farmers.
9. We never walk to the shop without money.
10. The sailors are sailing around the island.

LESSON 74

1. *The sailors' homeland*
2. *The girls' school*
3. *I am carrying the poets' writing tablets.*
4. *The women and the girls are in the boat with the sailors.*
5. *The poet is counting the stars.*
6. *The women are sailing around the island in boats.*
7. *The farmer's money is in the forest.*
8. *The girl is walking from the school to the shop.*
9. *You love the forest but the girls love the seashore.*
10. *Y'all are in the water without a boat.*

LESSON 75

1. *The farmer's family is in the house.*
2. *The sailors' families are on the island.*
3. *The woman's family is in the forest.*
4. *The sailors often sail to the homeland with money.*
5. *You are a poet but I am a farmer.*
6. *I never walk into the shop without money.*
7. *Y'all sail to the island daily.*
8. *Y'all are not near the island.*
9. *We are on the island without boats.*
10. *The farmers are longing for the homeland.*

LESSON 76

1. *I love the farmer's stories.*
2. *The girls do not like the sailor's story.*
3. *The farmer likes the sailors' boats.*
4. *The girl is in the school but she is longing for the seashore.*
5. *The sailors are carrying the boat to the water.*
6. *The farmer's family is walking to the shop.*
7. *The sailors are on the island without boats and without money.*
8. *You never carry water but I always carry water.*
9. *We always plow the soil but y'all are always in the house.*
10. *We are not sailing around the island.*

LESSON 77

1. *You are an inhabitant of the island.*
2. *There are inhabitants on the islands.*
3. *The inhabitants of the islands are swimming in the water.*
4. *The sailors are watching the inhabitants of the island.*
5. *The inhabitants of the forest walk to the seashore daily.*
6. *The inhabitants of the forest love stories.*
7. *The poet's family is longing for the homeland.*
8. *The girls carry writing tablets to school daily.*
9. *The girls are walking into the house.*
10. *You are sailing to the island with the sailors.*

LESSON 78

1. *I am telling a story.*
2. *The farmer is telling a story.*
3. *The sailors are telling stories.*
4. *We love the sailor's stories.*
5. *The sailors are on the island and they are telling stories.*
6. *The inhabitants of the island are swimming near the seashore.*
7. *Both the farmer and the poet are walking to the shop.*
8. *Y'all love boats but y'all are not sailors.*
9. *The boat is carrying the sailors' families to the island.*
10. *The sailors' boat is in the water.*

LESSON 79

1. money (direct object) friend (indirect object)
2. money (direct object) charity (indirect object)
3. example (direct object) class (indirect object)
4. curtains (direct object) house (indirect object)
5. seeds (direct object) garden (indirect object)
6. sandwiches (direct object) us (indirect object)
7. story (direct object) judge (indirect object)
8. song (direct object) audience (indirect object)
9. copies (direct object) everyone (indirect object)
10. shirt (direct object) me (indirect object)

LESSON 80

1. *I am telling a story to the sailor.*
2. *The poet is telling a story to the farmer.*
3. *The girls are telling stories to the poet.*
4. *The sailor's boat is in the water.*
5. *The inhabitants of the islands often swim in the water.*
6. *The girls' school is not in the forest.*
7. *You are a farmer but I am a poet.*
8. *The farmer's family is in the house.*
9. *I love the homeland but I am sailing to the island.*
10. *We are inhabitants of the forest but we love the seashore.*

LESSON 81

1. *We are telling stories to the sailors.*
2. *The sailor is telling a story to the farmers.*
3. *The poets are telling a story to the girl.*
4. *The women are in the forest.*
5. *The inhabitants of the islands love boats.*
6. *The poet is walking into the shop without money.*
7. *You always carry money.*
8. *The sailors are sailing around the island in boats.*
9. *The girls are in the school but they are longing for both the seashore and the forest.*
10. *We always plow the soil but y'all are always in the forest.*

LESSON 82

1. *I am giving money to the farmer.*
2. *The poet is giving writing tablets to the girls.*
3. *We are giving water to the inhabitants of the island.*
4. *The woman is giving writing tablets to the girls.*
5. *We are telling stories to the sailors.*
6. *I am swimming from the boat to the island.*
7. *The sailors' boat is in the water.*
8. *The girls always love stories.*
9. *Y'all are women.*
10. *Y'all often plow the soil.*

LESSON 85

1. *The farmer is building a house.*
2. *I am building a house and a boat.*
3. *Y'all are building a house on the island.*
4. *The poet is giving money to the sailors.*
5. *The girls always carry writing tablets to school.*
6. *The woman is in the house but the farmer is in the forest.*
7. *You are a sailor but you do not like the water.*
8. *We are building houses near the seashore.*
9. *The sailors' boat is on the island.*
10. *Y'all are farmers.*

LESSON 84

1. *I love the seashore and the forest.*
2. *The women and the girls are walking to the seashore.*
3. *Y'all often carry money and writing tablets.*
4. *I am watching the stars and the moon.*
5. *The poet is telling a story to the sailors.*
6. *We are not near the homeland.*
7. *We do not often walk to the seashore.*
8. *We walk to the school with the girls daily.*
9. *The sailor loves the homeland but he is sailing to the islands.*
10. *You always give money to the poet.*

LESSON 86

1. *I am guarding the houses.*
2. *The sailors are guarding the island and the boats.*
3. *We are guarding the farmer's house.*
4. *Y'all are building houses and boats.*
5. *The boat is sailing to the island without sailors.*
6. *The poet is walking to the shop without money.*
7. *The boats are carrying the sailors from the island to the seashore.*
8. *Y'all are telling stories to the girls but I am building a house.*
9. *The farmers are giving water to the sailor.*
10. *The house is not near the forest.*

LESSON 87

1. *I am working in the house.*
2. *The women and the girls are working in the forest.*
3. *I am carrying water but y'all are not working.*
4. *We are working but y'all are swimming in the water.*
5. *The girl is working with the farmers.*
6. *You are longing for the homeland.*
7. *We never give money to the poets.*
8. *You are in the water but I am in the boat.*
9. *I am building a house.*
10. *The sailor is not in the farmer's house.*

LESSON 88

1. to wash
2. to play
3. This sentence does not contain an infinitive.
4. to be
5. to forgive
6. to return
7. to play
8. This sentence does not contain an infinitive.
9. to buy
10. This sentence does not contain an infinitive.

LESSON 89

1. *I love to watch the boats.*
2. *I do not like to plow the soil.*
3. *The girls do not want to walk to school.*
4. *The sailors love to sail to the islands.*
5. *The girls want to walk into the forest.*
6. *We want to build houses near the seashore.*
7. *The sailor is telling stories to the farmers.*
8. *We are working in the farmers' house.*
9. *I am giving money to the girls.*
10. *We are guarding the houses and the boats.*

LESSON 90

1. *I am able to swim.*
2. *I am not able to carry the boat.*
3. *I am able to sail to the island.*
4. *I am not able to walk to the island.*
5. *I am not able to swim in the forest.*
6. *The inhabitants of the forests are guarding the houses.*
7. *We want to sail to the homeland.*
8. *The poet loves to tell stories to the girls.*
9. *I love to count the money daily.*
10. *The sailor's money is in the boat.*

LESSON 91

1. *You are not able to swim to the island.*
2. *We are able to walk to the forest.*
3. *Y'all are not able to swim to the island.*
4. *I am not able to build a boat without money.*
5. *The sailor often tells stories to the girls.*
6. *The sailors' boat is near the seashore.*
7. *The girls are working in the house.*
8. *The girls' school is near the forest.*
9. *I love to watch the boats.*
10. *The sailors are guarding the islands.*

LESSON 94

1. *I have a boat because I am a sailor.*
2. *We plow the soil because we are farmers.*
3. *I am watching the moon and the stars because I am a sailor.*
4. *The poet is telling a story to the girls because the girls love stories.*
5. *The family is in the boat because they want to sail to the homeland.*
6. *Y'all are not able to sail to the homeland without money.*
7. *The farmers' houses are near the forest.*
8. *The sailor's money is in the boat.*
9. *The woman is walking into the shop with the girls.*
10. *We are giving money to the poet.*

LESSON 93

1. *I have money.*
2. *You have a boat.*
3. *The poet has a writing tablet.*
4. *We do not have money but the sailors have money.*
5. *Y'all have money.*
6. *We are not able to sail around the island.*
7. *You want to build a house near the seashore.*
8. *The poet is telling a story to the farmers and sailors.*
9. *The inhabitants of the islands often swim in the water.*
10. *Y'all are not able to sail to the island.*

LESSON 95

1. *There are beasts in the forest.*
2. *The beasts are not able to build houses.*
3. *We are not able to plow the soil without beasts.*
4. *The beasts of the forest do not have houses.*
5. *You are not a poet.*
6. *The girl is giving water to the farmers.*
7. *I love to plow the soil because I am a farmer.*
8. *The sailor's boat is on the island.*
9. *We are not able to plow the soil because we do not have beasts.*
10. *You are carrying writing tablets.*

LESSON 96

1. *I do not fear the beasts.*
2. *The inhabitants of the island fear the beasts.*
3. *The girl is walking in the forest because she does not fear the beasts.*
4. *I want to walk in the forest with the beasts.*
5. *The beasts do not fear the farmers.*
6. *The beasts do not fear the sailors but the sailors fear the beasts.*
7. *We are giving money to the poet because he does not have money.*
8. *You are not able to sail to the island because you do not have a boat.*
9. *I am in the farmer's house.*
10. *I do not like the water because I am not able to swim.*

LESSON 97

1. *We love the queen.*
2. *The inhabitants of the forests do not fear the queen.*
3. *The poet is telling stories to the queen.*
4. *The queen always gives money to the poets.*
5. *The farmers fear the beasts of the forest.*
6. *You are not able to swim because you are an inhabitant of the forest.*
7. *The farmer's family is walking to the seashore because they love to swim.*
8. *The sailor has a boat but he does not have money.*
9. *I am not able to build a house without money.*
10. *The girls are carrying writing tablets because they are walking to the school.*

LESSON 98

1. *We see the island.*
2. *Y'all are not able to see the queen.*
3. *I see beasts daily because I am an inhabitant of the forest.*
4. *The inhabitants of the forests do not fear the beasts.*
5. *We are not able to guard the island without boats.*
6. *You are not the queen.*
7. *The farmer has a house in the forest.*
8. *The sailors fear the inhabitants of the islands.*
9. *The boats often sail around the island.*
10. *Beasts never carry money.*

LESSON 99

1. *The sailor is longing to stay on the island.*
2. *The beasts are staying in the forest.*
3. *You are not able to stay in the water.*
4. *I want to guard the homeland because I am the queen.*
5. *The sailors are staying on the island because they do not have a boat.*
6. *I see the stars but I am not able to see the moon.*
7. *The sailors do not fear the water because they are able to swim.*
8. *The inhabitants of the forest see beasts daily.*
9. *We never walk into the shop without money.*
10. *Y'all are not able to tell stories because y'all are not poets.*

LESSON 101

1. *I am a man.*
2. *The man is an inhabitant of the island.*
3. *The man has a house but he does not have a boat.*
4. *The man fears the beasts.*
5. *The man is telling stories to the inhabitants of the islands.*
6. *The man wants to stay on the island.*
7. *Y'all are walking to the shop but y'all do not have money.*
8. *You are a man but I am a woman.*
9. *We are not able to see the island.*
10. *Y'all are sailing from the homeland to the island.*

LESSON 102

1. *The men are in the house.*
2. *The men of the island are guarding the boats.*
3. *The man is not able to sail to the island without a boat.*
4. *The man and the woman often plow the soil.*
5. *Y'all are poets but y'all do not like to tell stories.*
6. *The beasts of the forests do not fear the farmers.*
7. *You are sailing to the homeland but I am staying on the island.*
8. *We see the stars but we are not able to see the moon.*
9. *The queen does not fear the inhabitants of the islands.*
10. *The queen always gives money to the poets.*

LESSON 103

1. *The beast does not fear the man.*
2. *I see men in the boat.*
3. *The man fears the beasts but the beasts do not fear the man.*
4. *The men are building houses.*
5. *The men never have money.*
6. *I am not able to build a house but I often build boats.*
7. *I am walking to the seashore with the girls.*
8. *The poet is telling stories to the girl.*
9. *The men of the islands often give boats to the sailors.*
10. *We are staying on the island because we love the island.*

LESSON 104

1. *The man's house is near the seashore.*
2. *The men's families are sailing to the island.*
3. *The man's boat is on the island.*
4. *The men in the boats are sailors.*
5. *The man is building a house on the island.*
6. *The men are not plowing the soil because they do not like to work.*
7. *The poet wants a writing tablet but he does not have money.*
8. *The queen is giving money to the poet.*
9. *The poet wants to stay with the queen.*
10. *The girl is carrying writing tablets to the school.*

LESSON 105

1. *I am telling a story to the man.*
2. *The queen is giving money to the men.*
3. *We want to work in the forest with the men.*
4. *The girl often gives water to the men.*
5. *You are not able to walk from the homeland to the island.*
6. *The men's boat is near the seashore.*
7. *The men of the forest do not like the farmer.*
8. *You are building a house on the island but I am building a house in the forest.*
9. *The girls walk from the school to the shop daily.*
10. *I never walk into the school without a writing tablet.*

LESSON 106

1. *I am building a wall.*
2. *We are building a wall around the houses.*
3. *The men are building walls.*
4. *The girl loves the homeland but she wants to sail to the islands.*
5. *I am not able to give money to the men and women of the island because I do not have money.*
6. *I am staying with the boats because I fear the men of the islands.*
7. *Y'all love to build boats but y'all do not like to sail.*
8. *I am in the house because I fear the beasts.*
9. *The boat is in the water without sailors.*
10. *We are not able to guard the homeland without the queen.*

LESSON 107

1. *The farmers are destroying the forest.*
2. *I am longing to destroy the houses and boats of the islands.*
3. *You are not able to destroy the sailors' boats because the sailors are guarding the boats.*
4. *The men are longing to guard the homeland.*
5. *The beasts of the forest are destroying the house.*
6. *We are guarding the men and women of the homeland.*
7. *The queen is not able to give money to the man because she does not have money.*
8. *The man's house is near the seashore.*
9. *I want to swim from the island to the homeland.*
10. *We are walking to the school with the girls.*

LESSON 108

1. *We are carrying food.*
2. *I have food but I do not have water.*
3. *I am carrying food and water.*
4. *The men are carrying food and water because they are walking to the forest.*
5. *The women are giving food to the poet because he does not have food.*
6. *The sailors do not have food.*
7. *The men of the islands are destroying the sailors' boats.*
8. *We are building a wall because we want to guard the homeland.*
9. *The queen always gives money to the men of the forest.*
10. *The beasts of the forest want food.*

LESSON 109

1. *The man's son is in the house.*
2. *The sailors are telling stories to the farmer's son.*
3. *The farmers' sons are plowing the soil.*
4. *The sailor's sons want to sail to the islands.*
5. *The girl is giving water to the farmer's sons.*
6. *We are not able to sail to the island without food and water.*
7. *The queen wants to stay on the island because she fears the men of the homeland.*
8. *I love to swim because I do not fear the water.*
9. *You are not able to sail to the island without a boat.*
10. *The men's houses are near the seashore.*

LESSON 110

1. *The boy is the poet's son.*
2. *The poet is giving writing tablets to the boys.*
3. *The boys are carrying water but they do not like to plow the soil.*
4. *The boys want to sail to the island but they do not have a boat.*
5. *I am not able to work in the forest because I fear the beasts.*
6. *We are not able to plow the soil without the farmer's sons.*
7. *We are telling stories to the boys.*
8. *I want food and water.*
9. *The boys are sailing to the island with the sailors.*
10. *The man is not able to see the moon because he is in the house.*

LESSON 111

1. *The boys are plowing the fields because the farmer is not able to work.*
2. *The farmer's sons are walking from the house to the field.*
3. *The boys want money but they do not like to plow the fields.*
4. *The beasts of the forest are destroying the farmers' houses.*
5. *The men fear the beasts but the beasts do not fear the men.*
6. *I want to stay on the island.*
7. *We are building a wall around the houses because we want to guard the men and women of the homeland.*
8. *There are farmers and boys in the fields.*
9. *I am not able to sail to the island because I do not have a boat.*
10. *We are not able to sail to the island without the sailors.*

LESSON 112

1. *I have a sword.*
2. *The men have swords.*
3. *The men and women have swords but they are not able to guard the fields.*
4. *The inhabitants of the islands have swords but we have boats.*
5. *We guard the fields and houses daily.*
6. *The beasts of the forest do not fear the farmer.*
7. *The boy is the queen's son.*
8. *You are not able to stay on the island because you do not have food.*
9. *The sailors are with the inhabitants of the island.*
10. *We guard the homeland daily because we love the queen.*

LESSON 115

1. *I am walking into the town.*
2. *The sailors are in the town.*
3. *The men want to build a wall around the town.*
4. *The poet is telling stories to the boys and girls of the town.*
5. *The men want to guard the walls of the town.*
6. *The men of the town have swords.*
7. *Y'all are boys but we are men.*
8. *We cannot guard the town because the town does not have walls.*
9. *The farmer's son never plows the fields because he does not like to work.*
10. *The men of the forest never build boats.*

LESSON 116

1. *I want gold.*
2. *The men of the forest do not have gold.*
3. *We are sailing to the homeland with money and gold.*
4. *The sailors are destroying the towns of the island because they want gold.*
5. *The boys and girls of the town do not like to plow the fields.*
6. *We are guarding the town because we fear the inhabitants of the islands.*
7. *We often give food to the poet's sons because they do not have money.*
8. *The poet often tells stories to the queen's sons.*
9. *The queen's son has money and gold but he wants to work in the fields with the farmers.*
10. *You are not able to swim around the island.*

LESSON 117

1. *I love silver and gold.*
2. *The sailors are carrying gold to the homeland.*
3. *We are carrying silver from the boat to the house.*
4. *The boys are working in the fields with the men of the town.*
5. *The queen wants to destroy the town.*
6. *The inhabitants of the towns fear the beasts of the forest.*
7. *Y'all have gold and silver but y'all do not have food.*
8. *We cannot build houses without money.*
9. *The queen wants to build a wall around the town.*
10. *The boys are swimming because they do not like to work.*

LESSON 118

1. *I am watching the sky.*
2. *There are stars in the sky.*
3. *The sailors always watch the sky.*
4. *You are never able to count the stars in the sky.*
5. *The island has gold and silver.*
6. *We are not able to see the sky because we are in the house.*
7. *The inhabitants of the towns fear the beasts.*
8. *I am staying in the house.*
9. *You are not able to sail to the island without a boat.*
10. *The boats are carrying food to the island.*

LESSON 119

1. *We are giving gifts to the queen.*
2. *The girls and boys are giving gifts to the sailors.*
3. *The men and women of the town always give money to the queen.*
4. *The girls want to give gifts to the queen.*
5. *The sailor's gift is in the boat.*
6. *The farmer's sons are plowing the fields because they want food and money.*
7. *You are not the queen.*
8. *The moon is in the sky.*
9. *I want to stay with the men of the town.*
10. *The boats are near the seashore.*

LESSON 123

1. *The men are fighting with swords and shields.*
2. *I do not like to fight.*
3. *The inhabitants of the island cannot fight because they do not have swords.*
4. *We have swords and shields because we are guarding the town.*
5. *I love to watch the stars in the sky.*
6. *The queen's son wants a sword.*
7. *I am walking to the seashore because I want to see the boats.*
8. *Y'all do not have food because y'all never plow the fields.*
9. *You are the farmer's son but I am the son of the queen.*
10. *I always watch the moon and the stars.*

LESSON 122

1. *The boy has a shield.*
2. *I am guarding the queen with a sword and shield.*
3. *We have swords and shields because we are guarding the walls of the town.*
4. *We are not able to guard the homeland without swords and shields.*
5. *I love silver and gold but I do not have money.*
6. *The inhabitants of the homeland are building houses.*
7. *I am sailing to the island by boat.*
8. *The men of the town do not like the queen's son.*
9. *We are longing to see the homeland.*
10. *The men of the islands want to destroy the homeland.*

LESSON 124

1. *I am carrying the wood into the house.*
2. *I am building a house with wood.*
3. *I do not like to carry wood.*
4. *We are carrying wood from the forest to the town.*
5. *I want to see the queen.*
6. *The men are guarding the homeland with swords.*
7. *We are building a wall around the town because we fear the beasts.*
8. *The sailors are building boats with wood.*
9. *We are giving gifts to the girls of the town.*
10. *You are not able to plow the fields without food and water.*

LESSON 125

1. *We are carrying rocks.*
2. *We are building a wall with rocks and wood.*
3. *The men are not able to build a house without wood and rocks.*
4. *The men of the island are destroying the towns of the homeland.*
5. *We are carrying rocks to the town because we are building a wall.*
6. *You do not have food because you do not like to work.*
7. *The men of the homeland fight with swords and shields daily.*
8. *The men and women are giving gold and silver to the queen.*
9. *The men have swords and shields because they are guarding the towns of the homeland.*
10. *You are sailing to the homeland but I am staying on the island.*

LESSON 127

1. *The woman is strong.*
2. *The man is strong.*
3. *The wood is strong.*
4. *The strong boys are plowing the fields.*
5. *The strong women are carrying water.*
6. *We are building a strong wall.*
7. *I am staying with the strong men of the homeland.*
8. *The strong girl often carries wood.*
9. *The men and boys of the town are carrying wood and rocks because they want to build a strong wall.*
10. *You do not fear the beast because you have a sword and a shield.*

LESSON 129

1. *The girls are happy.*
2. *The sailor is not happy.*
3. *The farmer is plowing the field with the strong beasts.*
4. *The poet is telling stories to the happy boys.*
5. *The farmer's family is happy because they have food and money.*
6. *The farmer's sons are strong but they do not like to work.*
7. *I love to watch the stars in the sky.*
8. *Y'all are not able to plow the fields without strong men.*
9. *The girls are happy because they are walking to the seashore.*
10. *The queen is not happy because the beasts are destroying the homeland.*

LESSON 130

1. *The farmer's son is a bad boy.*
2. *The bad queen wants to destroy the farmers' houses.*
3. *The bad boys never work in the fields.*
4. *The poet does not like bad stories.*
5. *The bad men are not able to destroy the town because we are guarding the town.*
6. *The strong women are carrying rocks from the fields to the seashore.*
7. *We want to see the queen because we do not have food.*
8. *The bad boys fight often.*
9. *Y'all are not able to stay on the island without food and water.*
10. *The men and women are giving gifts to the queen.*

LESSON 131

1. *The queen's bad daughter wants to destroy the homeland.*
2. *The farmer's daughters are strong because they carry water daily.*
3. *The men of the town are building a house with wood and rocks.*
4. *The boys of the homeland do not like to fight but they want to guard the homeland.*
5. *The farmer is not happy because he is not able to plow the field.*
6. *We are building a house with wood.*
7. *The poet is telling stories to the farmer's daughters.*
8. *I am guarding the sons and daughters of the queen.*
9. *The bad queen never gives gifts to the men and women of the homeland.*
10. *We are strong because we have swords and shields.*

LESSON 132

1. *The queen's son is a great man.*
2. *The great men of the homeland are guarding the town.*
3. *You are not able to stay on the large island because you do not have food.*
4. *The homeland has a great queen.*
5. *The sailor has a large family.*
6. *The farmer's house is not large.*
7. *We are watching the sky because we love to see the stars.*
8. *The strong boys are working in the fields but they are not happy.*
9. *The great beasts of the forests are destroying the farmers' houses.*
10. *The sailors always give money to the inhabitants of the island.*

LESSON 133

1. *I want to conquer the great islands because they have silver and gold.*
2. *The queen's bad sons are conquering the forest.*
3. *We are conquering the inhabitants of the islands with swords and shields.*
4. *The men of the islands are conquering the homeland.*
5. *A strong wall is guarding the town.*
6. *The men and women of the homeland are not happy because they never have food.*
7. *You are not able to fight the great men of the forest without food and water.*
8. *We always give gifts to the queen of the islands.*
9. *The queen's sons are guarding the towns because they love the homeland.*
10. *I do not like to work in the fields but I plow the fields daily.*

LESSON 134

1. *We have much silver.*
2. *We are not able to conquer the islands without many boats.*
3. *The homeland has many towns.*
4. *I want to build a strong wall with large rocks.*
5. *We are not able to plow the fields without many farmers.*
6. *The sailor loves the queen's daughter.*
7. *The queen's daughters are happy because they have much gold.*
8. *There are many women on the island.*
9. *We are giving many gifts to the queen's daughters.*
10. *The queen has many sons.*

CLASSICAL
PRONUNCIATION GUIDE

This abbreviated guide to classical pronunciation will provide a few of the most important points to keep in mind when adopting a classical pronunciation of Latin.

CONSONANTS

c always sounds like the **c** in *cat*, never like the **c** in *ceiling*
g always sounds like the **g** in *garden*, never like the **g** in *gelatin*
s is always a hissing sound as in *pass*, never a z sound as in *is*
t always sounds like the **t** in *time*, never a **sh** sound like the **t** in *promotion*
v always sounds like the **w** in *wild*, never like the **v** in *violin*

In Latin, the letter *i* is used two ways. First, it is used as a vowel (see vowel chart below). Second, it is sometimes used as a consonant before a vowel. When you see the letter *i* before a vowel, it sounds like a *y*. For instance, the Latin word **iam** is pronounced *yahm*. In some Latin textbooks, the letter *i* is replaced with the letter *j* when used as a consonant. So, the word **iam** would be written **jam**, but is still pronounced the same way.

VOWELS

In Latin, there are short vowels and long vowels. Long vowels have a mark over them. This mark is called a *macron*. Short vowels do not have a mark.

LONG VOWELS

ā sounds like the **a** in *father*
ē sounds like the **a** in *play*
ī sounds like the **e** in *me*
ō sounds like the **o** in *no*
ū sounds like the **u** in *tube*

SHORT VOWELS

a sounds like the **a** in *art*
e sounds like the **e** in *net*
i sounds like the **i** in *it*
o sounds like the **o** in *hot*

u sounds like the **u** in *put*

DIPHTHONGS (COMBINATIONS OF VOWELS)

ae is pronounced like the word *eye*
au is pronounced like the **ou** in *mouse*

ECCLESIASTICAL PRONUNCIATION GUIDE

This abbreviated guide to ecclesiastical pronunciation will provide a few of the most important points to keep in mind when adopting an ecclesiastical pronunciation of Latin.

CONSONANTS

c always sounds like the **c** in *cat*, except when it comes before **e, i, ae,** or **oe**. In these cases, it sounds like the **ch** in *cheese*.
g sounds like the **g** in *garden* when it comes before a consonant or before **a, o,** or **u**. When it comes before **e, i, y, ae** or **oe**, it sounds like the **g** in *gelatin*.
g and **n** together sound like the **ny** in *canyon*.
r is lightly rolled. **v** always sounds like the **v** in *violin*

VOWELS

The type of ecclesiastical pronunciation used in this book does not distinguish between long and short vowels with regard to quality of sound.

ā and **a** both sound like the **a** in *father*
ē and **e** both sound like the **e** in *bet*
ī and **i** both sound like the **e** in *me*
ō and **o** both sound like the **o** in *no*
ū and **u** both sound like the **u** in *tube*

DIPHTHONGS (COMBINATIONS OF VOWELS)

ae is pronounced like the **e** in *bet*
au is pronounced like the **ou** in *mouse*

GLOSSARY

ā, ab *from* (lesson 68)

acta *seashore* (lesson 52)

ad *to, toward* (lesson 51)

aedificō *I build* (lesson 85)

ager *field* (lesson 111)

agricola *farmer* (lesson 6)

ambulō *I walk* (lesson 50)

amō *I love, I like* (lesson 43)

aqua *water* (lesson 41)

argentum *silver* (lesson 117)

arō *I plow* (lesson 49)

aurum *gold* (lesson 116)

bestia *beast* (lesson 95)

caelum *sky* (lesson 118)

casa *house* (lesson 53)

cibus *food* (lesson 108)

circum *around* (lesson 57)

cotīdiē *daily* (lesson 67)

cum *with* (lesson 69)

deleō *I destroy* (lesson 107)

dēsīderō *I long for, I want* (lesson 61)

dō *I give* (lesson 82)

donum *gift* (lesson 119)

ego *I* (lesson 5)

es *you are* (lesson 11)

est *he is, she is, it is, is, there is* (lessons 13, 14, 66)

estis *y'all are* (lesson 18)

et *and* (lesson 8)

fābula *story* (lesson 76)

familia *family* (lesson 75)

fēmina *woman* (lesson 38)

fīlius *son* (lesson 109)

fīlia *daughter* (lesson 131)

gladius *sword* (lesson 112)

habeō *I have* (lesson 93)

in *in, on, into* (lesson 63)

incola *inhabitant* (lesson 77)

īnsula *island* (lesson 56)

labōrō *I work* (lesson 87)

laetus, laeta, laetum *happy* (lesson 129)

lignum *wood* (lesson 124)

lūna *moon* (lesson 27)

māgnus, māgna, māgnum *great, large* (lesson 132)

malus, mala, malum *bad* (lesson 130)

maneō *I stay* (lesson 99)

multus, multa, multum *many, much* (lesson 134)

murus *wall* (lesson 106)

narrō *I tell* (lesson 78)

nauta *sailor* (lesson 1)

natō *I swim* (lesson 58)

nāvigō *I sail* (lesson 55)

nōn *not* (lesson 10)

numerō *I count* (lesson 35)

numquam *never* (lesson 46)

oppidum *town* (lesson 115)

patria *homeland* (lesson 60)

pecūnia *money* (lesson 36)

poēta *poet* (lesson 12)

portō *I carry* (lesson 37)

possum *I am able* (lesson 90)

prope *near* (lesson 59)

puella *girl* (lesson 42)

puer *boy* (lesson 110)

pugnō *I fight* (lesson 123)

-que *and* (lesson 84)

quod *because* (lesson 94)

rēgīna *queen* (lesson 97)

saepe *often* (lesson 34)

saxum *rock* (lesson 125)

scapha *boat* (lesson 45)

schola *school* (lesson 65)

scutum *shield* (lesson 122)

sed *but* (lesson 48)

semper *always* (lesson 39)

servō *I guard* (lesson 86)

silva *forest* (lesson 44)

sine *without* (lesson 71)

spectō *I watch* (lesson 24)

stella *star* (lesson 26)

sum *I am* (lesson 3)

sumus *we are* (lesson 17)

superō *I conquer* (lesson 133)

sunt *they are, are, there are* (lesson 19, 66)

taberna *shop* (lesson 70)

tabula *writing tablet* (lesson 40)

terra *earth, land, soil* (lesson 47)

timeō *I fear* (lesson 96)

videō *I see* (lesson 98)

validus, valida, validum *strong* (lesson 127)

vir *man* (lesson 101)

SUBJECT INDEX

A

ablative, lesson 62

ablative of means, lesson 121

adjectives, lesson 126

adverb, lesson 34

article, lesson 2

C

case, lesson 54

conjugation, lesson 92

D

declension, lesson 100

definite article, lesson 2

direct object, lesson 22, 23

G

gender, lesson 113

genitive, lesson 73

genitive stem, lesson 111

I

indefinite article, lesson 2

indirect object, lesson 79

infinitive, lesson 88

instrument, lesson 120

M

means, lesson 120

N

negative, lesson 10

neuter nouns of the second declension, lesson 114

P

PAIN words, lesson 113, 128

person, lesson 21

plural, lesson 15

possessive, lesson 72

preposition, lesson 51

S

second declension, lesson 101

singular, lesson 15

subject, lesson 7

V

verb, lesson 9

W

word order, lesson 4